lonely  planet

POCKET

IBIZA

TOP EXPERIENCES • LOCAL LIFE

ISABELLA NOBLE

Contents

Plan Your Trip

Ibizan windmill
KAROL KOZLOWSKI/SHUTTERSTOCK ©

Explore Ibiza 29

COVID-19

We have re-checked every business in this book before publication to ensure that it is still open after the COVID-19 outbreak. However, the economic and social impacts of COVID-19 will continue to be felt long after the outbreak has been contained, and many businesses, services and events referenced in this guide may experience ongoing restrictions. Some may be temporarily closed, have changed their opening hours and services, or require bookings; some unfortunately could have closed permanently. We suggest you check with venues before visiting for the latest information.

Survival Guide 145

Special Features

Ibiza's Top Experiences

EIVAISLA/GETTY IMAGES ©

Wander the Medieval Lanes of Dalt Vila

Ibiza's World Heritage–listed old town. **p32**

ALEXANDRE G. ROSA/SHUTTERSTOCK ©

See the Sparkling Ses Salines Salt Pans

White-sand beaches; protected salt pans. **p66**

Pack an Umbrella for the Trucador Peninsula Beaches

Spain's top beaches; nature reserve. **p132**

NAEBLYS/SHUTTERSTOCK ©

Discover the Myths of Es Vedrà & its Surrounds

The Balearics' most magical natural islet. **p62**

LUKASZ JANYST/SHUTTERSTOCK ©

ANNAPURNA MELLOR/LONELY PLANET ©

Catch a Fabulous Sunrise on the Northern Beaches

Northern Ibiza's must-see beaches. **p98**

Shop Sant Carles de Peralta's Hippy Market

Low-key village; famous hippy market. **p96**

Climb to the 16th-Century Fortress-Church Puig de Missa

Santa Eulària's hilltop and fortress-church. **p82**

Venture Out to Sant Antoni's Coastal Surrounds

Glorious blonde beaches with *chiringuitos* (beach bars). **p118**

TRAVELLIGHT/SHUTTERSTOCK ©

MASSIMO DALLAGLIO/ALAMY STOCK PHOTO ©

Dance the Night Away in Sant Rafel de Sa Creu

Two legendary superclubs; traditional village. **p56**

Soak up the Summer Scene in the Port Area

Ibiza Town's ultra-lively harbour-front area. **p36**

MICHAL BEDNAREK/500PX ©

PILGUI/SHUTTERSTOCK ©

Bask on the Beaches of Botafoc & Talamanca

Glitzy marina; golden family-friendly beach. **p40**

Beaches

Ibiza is blessed with an astonishing number of beautiful beaches. There are white-sand wonders with luxury beach clubs, plus glorious undeveloped stretches of blonde sands inside natural parks. You'll find pretty coves dotted all along the Ibizan and Formenteran coasts, with some of the most secluded scattered around northern Ibiza.

Best Blissful White-Sand Beaches

Platja de Ses Salines Backed by dunes and thickets of pines, this popular, protected southeast-Ibiza beach has a raw, natural beauty, plus fabulous *chiringuitos* (beach bars). (p67)

Trucador Peninsula The glorious back-to-back, snow-white sands on Formentera's northernmost tip, Platja Illetes and Platja Llevant, are lapped by Caribbean-esque turquoise water. (p132)

Platja de Migjorn Hugging southern Formentera, this salt-hued haven is washed by aqua waves and sprinkled with barefoot-style *chiringuitos*. (p137)

Cala Saona A delightful soft-blonde cove tucked into western Formentera, with lovely sunset views. (p135)

Es Cavallet (p73) This white-sand beauty is Ibiza's most gay-friendly beach, especially at its southern end around the **Chiringay** (p76) bar-restaurant.

Platges de Comte This cluster of sun-bleached beaches boasts some of Ibiza's clearest waters. (p119; pictured)

Platja d'en Bossa The less-developed southern end of this busy gold-white beach is quieter, fringed by dunes, and hosts several stylish bar-restaurants. (p78)

Cala Salada Enjoy powder-soft sand and aquamarine sea on this tiny cliff-flanked cove. (p119)

Best Delectable Coves

Cala Mastella Pines border a glittering, deep-set emerald bay with an outstanding waterside seafood shack, on Ibiza's northeast coast. (p87)

Benirràs Drumming ceremonies celebrate the sunset on Sundays at this hill-ringed, distinctly bohemian north-Ibiza beach. (p99)

Cala Xuclar A protected northern-Ibiza cove, home to an excellent seafood-fuelled *chiringuito*, plus good snorkelling, near Portinatx. (p103)

Cala d'Hort Magnificent Es Vedrà views, fine snorkelling and three popular seafood restaurants entice on this

SIMONA PAVAN/SHUTTERSTOCK ©

sand-and-pebble cove in southwest Ibiza. (p63)

Cala d'en Serra Off the beaten track in Ibiza's far northeast, this gorgeous sandy cove is encircled by wooded hills and headlands. (p99)

Best Wild Beaches

Es Portitxol One of Ibiza's most remote, undeveloped corners, this horseshoe-shaped bay lies below soaring hills and craggy cliffs on the northern coastline. (p103)

Aigües Blanques A slender stretch of golden sand huddled beneath northeast Ibiza's coastal cliffs, this wild, naturist beach is washed by ocean-fresh waves. (p99)

S'Estanyol The nearest un-touristed, tucked-away cove to Ibiza Town, with fishing huts and just one boho-glam shoreside *chiringuito*. (p46)

Cala Llentrisca Getting there is half the fun when it comes to this hidden south-Ibiza bay, a 10-minute hike from the nearest road below the lofty mass of Cap Llentrisca. (p73)

Port de Ses Caletes Sky-reaching cliffs and a handful of fishers' huts are likely to be your only companions at this refreshingly isolated pebbly cove in northeast Ibiza. (p103)

Top Tips

⊙ Sun loungers and umbrellas cost €6 to €12 to rent on most beaches – beach clubs charge more – so it's worth buying your own on arrival.

⊙ Rob Smith's *Secret Beaches Ibiza* (2015) is the definitive guide to the Ibizan coastline.

⊙ Between November and April there are almost no beach bus services; a hire car or bike is essential for exploration.

Rural Hotels

There are at least 30 rural hotels (agroturisme in Catalan; agroturismo in Spanish) in Ibiza, most of which are gorgeously converted, centuries-old farmhouses. None are especially remote, but their tranquility, character and beauty are a unique Balearics escapism experience. This does, of course, come at a cost.

Atzaró (☎971 33 88 38; www.atzaro.com; Carretera Santa Eulària–Sant Joan Km 15; r €420-545, ste €506-710; P✳☎☀) Combining Japanese Zen with tribal Africa and farmhouse Ibiza, Atzaró (pictured) is the ultimate in rural-Ibiza luxury, 3km southeast of Sant Llorenç. Its exquisite rooms feature new-wave design and comforts, plus private terraces, fireplaces or four-poster beds. Besides a well-regarded restaurant (set menu €30), there's a divine **spa** (day pass €70; ⏰10am-8pm) in fragrant Mediterranean gardens.

Can Xuxu (☎971 80 15 84; www.canxuxu.com; Carretera Sant Josep–Cala Tarida Km 4; incl breakfast r €250-560, ste €385-890; ⏰Apr-Oct; P✳☎☀) Owner Alex and his staff really make this luxe

rural hotel, doting on guests and preparing homemade food. It's set in a 150-year-old *finca* (rural estate), 4.5km northwest of Sant Josep and decked out with Asian inspiration, and there's a lovely, private pool area. Book one of the converted 19th-century Javanese teak houses.

Can Pere (☎971 19 66 00; www.canpereibiza.com; Carretera Jesús–Cala Llonga (PMV810-1) Km 7.5; incl breakfast r €194-288, ste €273-324; ⏰Easter–mid-Oct; P✳☎☀) Surrounded by pine woods, 3km northwest of Ibiza's Cala Llonga, Can Pere enjoys a spectacular, secluded hilltop location with sweeping panoramas from its bougainvillea-shaded pool. Rooms and suites are smartly presented with rustic-contemporary design, and there's a fine

(guests-only) Mediterranean restaurant.

Can Pujolet (☎971 80 51 70; www.canpujolet.com; incl breakfast r €215-325, apt €405-550; P✳☎☀) Enjoy peace and quiet at this hidden-away 18th-century *finca*, 2.5km northeast of Santa Agnès. The 10 rooms play up simple luxury, with terracotta-tiled floors, exposed stone, and terraces rising from olive groves. Lounge by the pool and hot tub, or feast on meals fuelled by the hotel's organic produce.

Can Talaias (☎971 33 57 42; http://cantalaias.net; Carretera Sant Carles–Cala Boix; incl breakfast r €180-290, ste €335-380; ⏰Apr-mid-Oct; P✳☎☀) The former home of English actor Terry-Thomas, and now run by his son, this beautifully renovated, pine-

JUAN MANUEL APARICIO DIEZ/SHUTTERSTOCK ©

fringed Ibizan *finca* stands atop a Mediterranean-view hill, 2km northeast of Sant Carles. It's one of the island's original *agroturismes*.

Can Curreu (☎971 33 52 80; www.cancurreu. com; Carretera Eivissa–Sant Carles Km 12; incl breakfast r €300-325, ste €430-605; P ❄ 🛜 ≋) Above terraces of almond and fruit trees, and amid close-clipped lawns bordered by a kaleidoscope of roses, this modernised Ibizan farmstead has 19 exquisitely furnished rooms, along with a smart restaurant (mains €22 to €30) and a multi-facility spa (included). It's 1.5km southwest of Sant Carles.

Es Pas (☎687 807819; www.espasformentera. com; Venda Ses Clotades; d €220-270, q €300-400; ⏰Mar-Oct; P ❄ 🛜 ≋)

West of Formentera's Es Caló bay, this 200-year-old country house enjoys a peaceful location from which you can walk to both north- and south-coast beaches. It has a delightful pool and gardens, while each of the eight white-washed rooms is done up with cosy modern style.

Can Planells (☎971 33 49 24; www.canplanells. com; Carrer de Venda Rubió 2, Sant Miquel de Balansat; r €200-250, ste €264-352; ⏰May-Oct; ❄ 🛜 ≋) This peaceful countryside mansion, 1.5km southwest of Sant Miquel, exudes relaxed rural luxury in its handful of tastefully arranged modern-rustic doubles and suites. The best have private terraces. Mellow out by the pool or in the gardens and fruit-tree groves. Farm-fresh

produce makes breakfast that bit special.

Can Fuster (www.hotel ruralibizacanfuster.com; Carrer d'Eivissa; incl breakfast s €65, d €115-125; ❄ 🛜 ≋) Sky-blue paintwork welcomes you at this charmingly restored 150-year-old Ibizan farmhouse in Sant Joan. The eight cosy, rustic rooms are adorned with wood beams and tiled floors. A pool glistens in the garden, and the family team deliver fresh breakfasts.

Can Gall (☎971 33 70 31; www.agrocangall.com; Carretera Eivissa-Sant Joan Km 17.2; incl breakfast d €242-297, f €451; P ❄ 🛜 ≋) This tranquil 200-year-old *finca* is set amid citrus and olive groves, 7km northeast of Sant Llorenç. Rooms are luxuriously rustic, and there's an, plus bikes for borrowing.

Dining Out

LAURAAG4/SHUTTERSTOCK ©

Ibiza is a wonderland of local and international flavours, with much of its cuisine fuelled by local, often-organic ingredients. Island specialities include sofrit pagès (country-meat fry-up); bullit de peix (fish stew), served with arròs a banda (paella-style rice in fish stock); and flaó, a cheesecake-like dessert.

Best for Seafood

El Bigotes Simple waterside meals. (p90)

Fish Shack A top seasonal Talamanca hut for fresh fish. (p51)

Es Torrent Pricey but superb *bullit de peix*, *fideuà* and rice dishes. (p77)

Es Boldadó With *that* view of Es Vedrà. (p74)

Best for Vegetarians

Giri Café Go seasonal, local, sustainable and organic at this café-restaurant. (p109)

Wild Beets Imaginative, organic vegan cuisine in Santa Gertrudis. (p101)

Passion Boho-glam, healthy-eating cafe with branches across Ibiza. (p48)

Locals Only Fresh, organic Italian-Mediterranean in Ibiza Town. (p47)

Best for Meat

Can Caus Expertly grilled local meats; moderate prices. (p112)

Ca'n Pilot Grill your own *chuletón* (T-bone steak) in Sant Rafel. (p57)

Cas Pagès A local island-meat experience. (p111)

Es Rebost de Can Prats Great Sant Antoni spot for Ibizan dishes. (p124)

Best Budget Eats

S'Escalinata Light meals on the steps in Dalt Vila. (p48)

Comidas Bar San Juan Excellent-value, no-frills Spanish cooking. (p48)

Racó Verd Sant Josep's favourite tapas, breakfast and live-music cafe-bar. (p79)

Best High-End

Amante Super-glam cliff-side restaurant. (p89)

La Paloma The perfect Italian-Ibizan restaurant. (p109)

Best *Chiringuitos*

Chiringuito Utopía Sardine barbecues in a tucked-away bay. (p110)

Chiringuito Cala Xuclar Simple north-coast fish shack. (p111)

Clubs

Believe the hype. Despite being, essentially, a tiny island in the western Mediterranean, Ibiza can lay claim to being the world's queen of clubs. Top DJs spin their magic here in summer, and the clubbing industry is very much the engine of the Ibizan economy. Sant Rafel, Ibiza Town, Platja d'en Bossa and Sant Antoni are the megaclub hubs.

SIMONA FLAMIGNI/SHUTTERSTOCK ©

Pacha Nowhere on the island matches this adored megaclub's class and style. (p52)

Amnesia Steeped in Ibizan clubbing history, mammoth Amnesia is where DJ Alfredo pioneered the Balearic Beat. (p57)

Ushuaïa The ultimate Ibiza daytime pool-party spot. (p78)

Hï Ibiza This ultraglam megaclub stars big-name DJs and neon light shows. (p78)

Privilege An Ibizan legend and the world's most colossal club. (p57; pictured)

DC 10 Swap celeb sightings and VIP areas for an underground vibe and music-savvy clubbing crowd. (p78)

Tipic Formentera's one, fabulous club, in Es Pujols. (p142)

Top Tips

○ Discounted club tickets can be bought from authorised merchants, bars and promoters all over the island.

○ Drink prices in clubs are outrageous, typically €10 to €12 for beer or water, and €15 to €20 for a *combinado* (spirit and mixer). Local bars, particularly in Ibiza Town, offer more affordable drinks, and are great as a warm-up for the big clubs.

○ To cut clubbing transport costs, use the **Discobus** (p151); tickets cost €3 to €4 per person.

Historical Gems

Ibiza and Formentera have a fascinating history dating back to Phoenician times. Ibiza Town's historic walled city of Dalt Vila is a Unesco World Heritage site and contains several intriguing museums. Every village centres on a charming church, while along the islands' coastlines, evocative defence towers recall the once-omnipresent pirate threat.

IMAGEBROKER/ALAMY STOCK PHOTO ©

Best Museums

Centre d'Interpretació Madina Yabisa Hidden away up in Dalt Vila, this compact museum unravels Ibiza's Moorish period. (p34)

Necròpolis del Puig des Molins A fascinating Punic burial site (over 3000 tombs) and archaeological museum, near Ibiza Town's centre. (p46; pictured)

Museu d'Art Contemporani d'Eivissa Contemporary art with an island connection, plus archaeological finds, in a landmark building tucked into Dalt Vila. (p33)

Museu Etnogràfic Delve into traditional rural Ibizan life at this converted Santa Eulària farmhouse. (p83)

Best Churches

Catedral Ibiza Town's cathedral, built in Catalan Gothic style, crowns Dalt Vila. (p34)

Església de Puig de Missa Flaunting its own defence tower, this sparkling-white church-fortress gazes out on Santa Eulària. (p83)

Església de Sant Miquel A 14th-century fortified church in north Ibiza, with intricate murals and traditional dancing. (p106)

Església de Sant Llorenç This 18th-century northeast-Ibiza fortress-church is fronted by a porch and single entrance arch. (p106)

Església de Jesús A masterful Gothic altarpiece is the star at this 1466 church just north of Ibiza Town. (p48)

Best Defence Towers

Torre des Savinar Hike up to this 18th-century watchtower for unparalleled views over Es Vedrà and Ibiza's southern coastline. (p63)

Torre de Ses Portes Towers on the tip of southeast Ibiza, with vistas south to Formentera. (p67)

Torre d'en Valls Enjoys an isolated position in Ibiza's northeast, overlooking Tagomago. (p107)

Torre des Garroveret An 18th-century defence tower perched on Formentera's deep southern Cap de Barbària. (p135)

Bar Open

Ibiza Town's Port Area has dozens of fun seaside bars and is the island's main LGBTIQ+ hub, while Sant Antoni is home to Ibiza's legendary Sunset Strip bars (and more than a few British-style pubs). Dotted all over Ibiza and Formentera are wonderful chiringuitos, an ever-growing number of glitzy beach clubs and some delightfully local village bars.

SERGEY SIVKOV/SHUTTERSTOCK ©

Best Fashionable Bars

Experimental Beach Beachy, upmarket cocktail bar and restaurant overlooking Ibiza's salt pans. (p79)

Sunset Ashram Queen of Ibiza's boho-glam beach-bar scene, with fiery west-coast sunsets and DJ beats. (p127; pictured)

Bar 1805 A Sa Penya cocktail gem mixing up absinthe concoctions among its creative combinations. (p43)

Hostal La Torre Hit the coast north of Sant Antoni for uncommercial sunset vibes and big international DJs. (p126)

Pikes Recreate the Club Tropicana vibe at this legendary venue near Sant Antoni. (p127)

Best Local Bars

Bar Anita Sant Carles' most famous village watering hole; try the homemade *hierbas* liquor. (p115)

Bar Costa Art-splashed Santa Gertrudis bar for simple tapas and sensibly priced drinks. (p101)

Café Vista Alegre Murals adorn the terrace at this locally loved Sant Joan cafebar. (p111)

Fonda Pepe Boho bar with a lively countercultural history

in Formentera's Sant Ferran. (p142)

Madagascar One of Ibiza Town's best terraces. (p43)

Best Beach Bars

Sa Trinxa Salines beach's top *chiringuito* has a mellow ambience and Balearic sounds. (p79)

Beachouse Gaze over Platja d'en Bossa from a Bali bed while DJs take to the decks. (p76)

Chiringuito Bartolo A teensy, locally loved *chiringuito* hidden away on Formentera's Platja de Migjorn. (p142)

Under the Radar

Ibiza may attract a staggering seven million visitors a year (!), but, with a little effort, you'll always be able to hunt down a remote spot, if you have the inclination to prime your sense of discovery and leave the main roads behind.

NITO/SHUTTERSTOCK ©

Best Secret Coves

Caló des Moltons Invisible from northern Ibiza's Port de Sant Miquel, but actually just metres around the coast. (p103)

Port de Ses Caletes A rough-and-ready road leads to this hidden north-Ibiza cove of pebbles. (p103)

Es Portitxol Brave the 20-minute hike to this gloriously remote horseshoe bay northwest of Sant Miquel. (p103)

Es Torrent An idyllic little cove at the foot of a river valley on Ibiza's south coast. (p77)

Cala d'Aubarca Hoof it on foot to broad, exposed, 3km-wide Aubarca bay in Ibiza's northwest. (p103)

Cala Saladeta On Ibiza's west coast, Cala Salada's baby-sister cove is reached by scrambling past fishers' huts. (p119)

Best Offbeat Secret Spots

Far de Portinatx Accessed via a dramatic coastal hike, Portinatx lighthouse basks in distant views of Mallorca. (p105; pictured)

Stonehenge Andrew Rogers' extraordinary sculpture on a secluded rocky coastline in Ibiza's southwest. (p71)

Sant Francesc de s'Estany (p71) Blink and you'll miss this tiny settlement overlooking south Ibiza's salt pans. (p71)

Ses Feixes Crop-growing fields developed by the Moors on the edge of Ibiza Town. (p41)

Casita Verde A remote south-Ibiza ecocentre that promotes sustainable farming; private tours can be arranged. (p58)

Best Secret Caves

Cova des Culleram Intriguing cave-temple dedicated to the goddess Tanit, in far northeast Ibiza. (p105)

Cova de Buda Perched above Atlantis, this tricky-to-access cave contains a beautiful Buddha image. (p65)

Cova des Mirador Inspiring views from a cave below the main Es Vedrà lookout point. (p65)

For Families

Despite its rave-all-night reputation and couples-oriented hotels, Ibiza is actually a wonderful destination for families. The island isn't packed with sights specifically designed to entertain kids, but there are plenty of sheltered beaches, quiet villages, family-friendly hotels and restaurants to satisfy all tastes, plus the wonders of Dalt Vila to explore.

WESTEND61/GETTY IMAGES ©

Dalt Vila (p32) This mesmerising walled city feels like an enormous castle, with its stupendous defensive walls, ramparts, bastions, towers and **Portal de Ses Taules** (p33).

Boat trips An adventure over to Formentera makes a fantastic day out for the whole family. If you don't fancy a full day trip, catch a ride on one of the little summer water taxis that link Ibiza's main towns, resorts and beaches. (p150)

Aquarium Cap Blanc Just north of Sant Antoni, this small boardwalk-equipped aquarium hidden in a natural cave has a series of tanks containing local fish, octopuses, lobsters, moray eels and starfish, plus the odd turtle. (p123)

Platja de Talamanca Shallow waters and a smattering of excellent seaside restaurants make this golden beach, just east of Ibiza Town, a family favourite. (p41)

Cala Bassa If you're on the west side of Ibiza, this beautiful cove beach is well worth a visit with the kids; between the turquoise waves and blonde sand, you'll find activities aplenty, including pedalos for hire and banana-boat rides. (p119)

Outdoor activities Horse rides and kayaking excursions are perfect for holidaying families. (p20)

Top Tips

○ Many Ibizan restaurants don't open until 8pm in the evening, so plan accordingly if you have hungry mouths to feed.

○ Plenty of eateries offer kids' menus, with a short selection of simple, plain and unthreatening dishes at fair prices.

○ Ibiza has many adults-only hotels, but also excellent family-friendly options; do double-check when booking.

Active Ibiza

With a benign climate and sparkling, unpolluted waters, Ibiza offers plenty of opportunities for activity lovers. It's easy to rent a kayak, snorkel, paddleboard or bike, join a yoga class or horse-riding expedition, or just head off on a self-guided coastal hike.

GOODLUZ/SHUTTERSTOCK ©

Ibiza Horse Valley (www. ibizahorsevalley.com; ☺Fri-Wed) Near Sant Joan, this sanctuary for mistreated horses offers half-day hill treks (€80), full-day beach treks (€150) and horseback camping trips. The horses roam in semi-liberty and there's an important focus on bonding with them. Book ahead by email; minimum age 12.

Walking Ibiza (☎608 692901; www.walkingibiza. com) Hit Ibiza's trails with pro guide Toby and his multilingual team. Guided expeditions range from day hikes (€160 to €200) to two-week around-the-island treks (€1600). The team also runs excellent food tours (https:// ibizafoodtours.com).

Wet4Fun (☎971 32 18 09; www.wet4fun.com; Carrer

Roca Plana 51-69, Es Pujols; ☺10am-6pm Mon-Sat, 2-6pm Sun May-Oct) A professional Formentera water-sports outfit offering windsurfing, paddleboarding, catamaran sailing, canoeing and kayaking. You can rent kayaks (€23 per hour) and paddleboards (€20 per hour), head out on three-hour kayaking trips (per person €39), or try a two-hour SUP yoga class (€35).

Ibiza MTB (☎616 129929, 637 352929; www. ibizamtb.com; Carrer Joan Castelló 1, Sant Rafel de Sa Creu; ☺10am-1pm & 5-8pm Mon-Fri, 10am-1pm Sat) Ibiza has some fantastic mountain-bike terrain. Ibiza MTB rents bikes (per day €15 to €50), with helmets and roadside assistance

included. Or slip into the saddle for two- to three-hour guided mountain-bike tours.

Orcasub (☎971 80 63 07; www.orcasub.es; Insotel Tarida Beach Sensatori Hotel, Cala Tarida; dives from €50) These multilingual PADI professionals dive off Ibiza's southwestern coast at sites including Es Vedrà. Courses run from beginner immersions (€100) to open water (€410). Snorkelling boat trips (€35) are also offered.

Ibiza Mundo Activo (☎676 075704; http:// ibizamundoactivo.blog spot.co.uk) This one-stop adventure-sports shop takes you hiking, cycling, caving, climbing and kayaking across Ibiza.

Sunsets & Villages

Sunset is a big deal in Ibiza, essentially thanks to DJ José Padilla who spun his phenomenal downbeat sets for years as Café del Mar's resident DJ. For an authentic flavour of Balearic island life away from the resorts, drop by a few of Ibiza's charming villages. Each is graced by an attractive landmark church and is the focus of a wider rural community.

ANTON CALPAGIU/SHUTTERSTOCK ©

Best Ibiza Sunsets

Torre des Savinar The perfect spot to soak up the sunset over Es Vedrà. (p63)

Benirràs Top sunset choice in north Ibiza, especially for the Sunday drumming sessions. (p99; pictured)

Stonehenge Savour the sinking sun on Andrew Rogers' inspirational sculpture. (p71)

Sunset Strip Sant Antoni's classic sunset hangout. (p128)

Platges de Comte Islands speckle the horizon from these white, sunset-mad sands. (p119)

Ses Salines Ibiza's salt pans glitter in a kaleidoscopic palette of pinks at sunset. (p66)

Best Formentera Sunsets

Cap de Barbària The lunar-like landscape around this remote southern lighthouse adds drama to the occasion. (p135)

Cala Saona The cliffs around this beautiful bay are the perfect vantage point for sunset. (p135)

Best Villages

Sant Joan de Labritja Cottage-like houses, excellent bar-restaurants and a handful of secluded hotels make this a mandatory north-Ibiza stop. (p110)

Santa Gertrudis de Fruitera This lively interior-Ibiza village is known for its cafes, bars, restaurants and boutiques. (p100)

Sant Carles de Peralta This village in northeast Ibiza hosts famous **Bar Anita**, an 18th-century church, a smattering of boutiques and **Las Dalias** hippy market. (p96)

Sant Francesc Xavier Formentera's 'capital' has an array of barefoot-living boutiques and cafes to complement its village square and fortress-church. (p141)

Sant Josep de Sa Talaia (p71) South Ibiza's main hub appeals, with an imposing 18th-century church, good tapas bars and a buzzy cafe/music spot, **Racó Verd** (p79).

Santa Agnès de Corona Squirrelled away in Ibiza's northwest, this remote village revolves around a 19th-century church and a few restaurants. (p106)

Four Perfect Days

Day 1

Begin with an Ibizan breakfast at **Madagascar** (p43) in Ibiza Town, then climb the city's World Heritage–listed Dalt Vila to the hilltop Catalan Gothic **Catedral** (p34; pictured).

Head south to stunning **Platja de Ses Salines** (p67), pausing to admire the **Ses Salines salt pans** (p66), then catch some Balearic tunes and lunch at **Sa Trinxa** (p79). Alternatively, make for gorgeous **Es Cavallet** (p73), Ibiza's main gay beach. Then it's a spin west to catch the sunset over **Es Vedrà** (p62) from the isolated **Torre des Savinar** (p63) watchtower.

Hit Ibiza Town's buzzing **Port Area** (p36) bars for drinks and dinner at **Locals Only** (p47). Then, for anyone with the energy, it's the world-famous dance floor at **Pacha** (p52).

Day 2

Grab breakfast with a view at **Passion** (p48), then drive up the island's east coast via the **Església de Jesús** (p48) and **Cala Llonga** (p89). Next, explore the fortress-church and other sights of Santa Eulària's **Puig de Missa** (p82).

Continue north for the little cove of **Cala Mastella** (p87; pictured), with its impossibly scenic *chiringuito* **El Bigotes** (p90) jutting out into the water, or slender, wild **Aigües Blanques** (p99). Next, pop inland to the delightful white village of **Sant Carles de Peralta** (p96).

You can't beat the relaxed evening vibe around the pretty Santa Gertrudis village square. Swing by **Bar Costa** (p101) and dine on fine Italian at **Macao Cafe** (p101) or healthy-eating menus at **Wild Beets** (p101).

Day 3

Go to beautiful, beach-laden Formentera. Hire a bike or scooter at La Savina port, then head for the charming 'capital', **Sant Francesc Xavier** (p141). Find the **fortress-church** (p136) and grab a bite at **Ca Na Pepa** (p137). Next, spin north to the **Trucador Peninsula** (p132). If conditions are clear, you can wade over to the islet of **Espalmador** (p133).

In the afternoon, travel to La Mola peninsula, famous for its **lighthouse** (p135; pictured). Take a break at clifftop cafe **Codice Luna** (p137), before backtracking west to **Platja de Migjorn** (p137) for drinks at **Chiringuito Bartolo** (p142).

Fit in a drink or a meal on Platja de Migjorn, before catching a late ferry to Ibiza.

Day 4

Head to low-key northern Ibiza, stopping for breakfast at **Giri Café** (p109) and a peep at the **church** (p110) in the village of **Sant Joan** (p110). Then head north to **Portinatx** (p107) for a cliffside walk past electric-blue waters to its secluded **light-house** (p105).

Head west along the north coast to the lovely, sheltered, hippy-vibe cove of **Benirràs** (p99; pictured), surrounded by wooded hills and with several beachfront restaurants.

In the early evening, get a spa treatment at luxe hotel **Atzaró** (p107), before visiting Sant Llorenç's **La Paloma** (p109) for an Italian meal. Alternatively, head to the west coast for drinks on Sant Antoni's **Sunset Strip** (p128), and wrap up with dinner at **Cala Gracioneta** (p124).

Need to Know

For detailed information, see Survival Guide (p145)

Currency
Euro (€)

Languages
Spanish, Catalan

Visas
EU & Schengen countries No visa required.
UK, Australia, Canada, Israel, Japan, NZ & the US ETIAS pre-authorisation to be introduced in 2022 (www.etiasvisa.com).
Other countries Check with embassy.

Money
ATMs widely available. Credit cards widely accepted; some *chiringuitos* are cash only.

Mobile Phones
No data-roaming costs for EU mobile phones. Visitors from other countries may consider purchasing a local SIM.

Time
GMT/UTC plus one hour during winter and two hours during daylight saving (end of March to end of October).

Daily Budget

Budget: Less than €100
Guesthouse double room: €65–75
Bocadillo/tostada and self-catering from supermarkets: €10
Bus transport to beaches and villages: €1.65–4
Combinado (spirit and mixer) in basic bar: €8

Midrange: €100–200
Double room in comfortable hotel: €75–200
Rental car per day: from €20
Dinner with wine: €30–40
Cocktail in a beachfront bar: €12–15

Top end: More than €200
Double room at boutique hotel or *agroturisme*: from €200
Club entry: €30–70
Rental car per day: from €20
Combinado in club: €15–20
Gourmet dinner with wine: from €40

Advance Planning

Six months before Reserve accommodation, flights and car hire.

Two weeks before Book tables for restaurants.

Useful Websites

Turismo de Ibiza (http://ibiza.travel) Official island-wide tourism website.

Ibiza Spotlight (www.ibiza-spotlight.com) Recommendations, reviews, island guides.

Lonely Planet (www.lonelyplanet.com/spain/ibiza) Destination information, hotel reviews and more.

Arriving in Ibiza

✈ Aeroport d'Eivissa

From Ibiza's airport (www.aena. es; Sant Jordi de ses Salines), buses run to destinations across Ibiza, including Ibiza Town, Platja d'en Bossa, Sant Antoni, Sant Josep and Santa Eulària; rates are €3.50 to €4. Taxis cost €18 to Ibiza Town (around 15 minutes). Car-hire companies have offices at the airport or will meet you there.

Destination	Bus Route
Ibiza Town and Formentera Ferry Terminal	L10
Sant Antoni via Sant Josep	L9
Santa Eulària	L24
Platja d'en Bossa	L36

⚓ Estació Marítima de Botafoc, Ibiza Town

Most long-distance ferries arrive into Ibiza's Botafoc ferry terminal, across the harbour from central Ibiza Town. Buses, taxis and boats shuttle to and from the city centre.

⚓ La Savina, Formentera

All boats to Formentera arrive at the port of La Savina. You'll find rows of outlets renting bicycles, motorbikes and cars. Buses (p152) to/from villages across Formentera stop in La Savina, or you could hop in a taxi (p152).

Getting Around

The best way to get around Ibiza is undoubtedly by car, which gives you independence and the chance to reach remote destinations. Formentera is also best explored with your own wheels.

🚗 Car

For the best rates (and availability), book car hire well in advance. Motorbikes/scooters are good for easy parking at beaches in high season.

⚓ Ferry

Ibiza Town and Formentera's La Savina port are linked by regular ferries (every 20 to 30 minutes May to October, reduced services November to April).

🚌 Bus

If you're based in one of the main towns, Ibiza's and Formentera's bus networks are efficient and budget-friendly. If you're staying in the countryside or want to visit remote beaches, you may struggle to find regular buses (if any).

🚲 Bicycle

Formentera is mostly very flat, making it perfect for bikes. Ibiza is far more hilly, though it does have decent bike paths.

🚕 Taxi

Taxis are an excellent way to get around both islands, though costs can quickly add up and, in July and August, demand outstrips supply.

Ibiza Regions

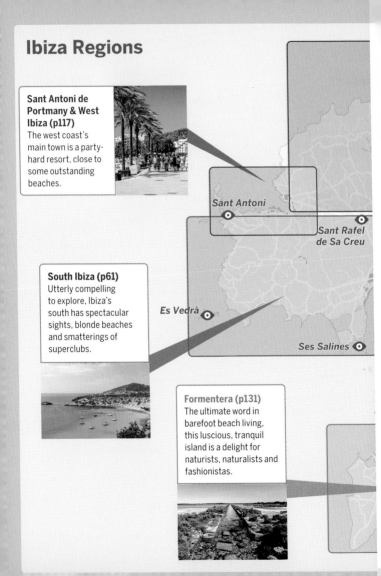

Sant Antoni de Portmany & West Ibiza (p117)
The west coast's main town is a party-hard resort, close to some outstanding beaches.

South Ibiza (p61)
Utterly compelling to explore, Ibiza's south has spectacular sights, blonde beaches and smatterings of superclubs.

Formentera (p131)
The ultimate word in barefoot beach living, this luscious, tranquil island is a delight for naturists, naturalists and fashionistas.

Sant Antoni

Sant Rafel de Sa Creu

Es Vedrà

Ses Salines

Northern Beaches

Northern Beaches

Northern Beaches

Northern Beaches

Sant Carles de Peralta

Puig de Missa

North & Interior Ibiza (p95)
Ibiza's less-developed north is all about wild nature, dramatic scenery, remote coves and bohemian villages.

Botofac & Talamanca

Dalt Vila & Port Area

Santa Eulària des Riu & East Ibiza (p81)
Eastern Ibiza is blessed with a sparkling coastline of unhurried beaches, while Santa Eulària town hosts some intriguing sights.

Trucador Peninsula

Ibiza Town & Around (p31)
The island's capital is historically fascinating, impossibly chic and a delight to explore.

Explore
Ibiza

Ibiza's Walking Tours 🥾

Ibiza's Driving Tours 🚗

Las Dalias (p115) GMANN PHOTOGRAPHY/500PX ©

Explore
Ibiza Town & Around

The island's heart and soul, Ibiza Town (Eivissa) is a vivacious, stylish and elegant capital with a magical, fortified World Heritage–listed old quarter topped by a castle and cathedral, all set against leafy squares, whitewashed lanes, fascinating museums and a spectacular natural harbour. It's also a shopaholic's dream, a hedonist's paradise and a world-famous party destination, home to some of the globe's glitziest megaclubs.

Plaça des Parc and Passeig de Vara de Rey are perfect spots to linger over a quintessential Ibizan break-fast before meandering up into the historic, World Heritage–listed Dalt Vila, exploring its museums, viewpoints, ramparts and cathedral.

Ibiza Town at night is something to behold. Depending on your mood, wander around the Port Area, dine at a sensational restaurant or bar-hop your way through packed-out Carrer de la Verge, Ibiza's LGBTIQ+ village, before hitting a megaclub.

Getting There & Around

🚌 L10 to/from airport (€3.50, 20 minutes, every 20 to 30 minutes).

🚌 L3 to/from Sant Antoni (€2, 25 minutes, every 15 to 30 minutes).

🚌 L13 to/from Santa Eulària (€2, 25 minutes, every 20 to 60 minutes).

Ibiza Town & Around Map on p44

Streets in Ibiza Town IVAN SMUK/SHUTTERSTOCK ©

Top Experience 📷
Wander the Medieval Lanes of Dalt Vila

Its formidable 16th-century bastions visible from across southern Ibiza, Dalt Vila is a fortified hilltop first settled by the Phoenicians then occupied by a roster of subsequent civilisations. Many of its cobbled, atmospheric lanes are accessible only on foot. It's mostly residential, but contains medieval mansions and several key cultural sights. All lanes lead to the cathedral-topped summit.

◉ MAP P44, D5

Bus L45 from Passeig de Vara de Rey to Dalt Vila (€1.65, hourly).

Ramparts

Entirely encircling Dalt Vila, Ibiza's colossal protective Renaissance-era **walls** tower over 25m in height, framed by seven bastions. Evocatively floodlit at night, these fortifications were constructed in the 16th century to protect Ibizans against the threat of attacks by North African raiders and the Turkish navy, and were designed to withstand heavy artillery. In less than an hour, you can walk the entire 2km perimeter, enjoying fabulous panoramas over the port and south across the water to Formentera.

Portal de Ses Taules

From Ibiza Town's market square, a stone ramp climbs to the majestic Portal de Ses Taules, the main entrance to Dalt Vila. The **gateway** is flanked by two statues, replicas from Ibiza's Roman era, which add to its grandeur. Above it hangs a plaque bearing Felipe II's coat of arms and an inscription recording the 1585 fortification completion date. You pass through into the elegant multi-arched **Pati d'Armes** (Armoury Courtyard), which once hosted the island's original hippy markets.

Museu d'Art Contemporani d'Eivissa

Set inside an 18th-century powder store and armoury, Dalt Vila's excellent **Museu d'Art Contemporani d'Eivissa** (MACE; www.eivissa. es/mace; Ronda de Narcís Puget; admission free; ⏰10am-2pm & 6-9pm Tue-Fri Jul & Aug, 10am-2pm & 5-8pm Tue-Fri Apr-Jun & Sep, 10am-4.30pm Tue-Fri Oct-Mar, 10am-2pm Sat & Sun year-round) is a showcase for contemporary art, most with an Ibizan connection. The permanent collection contains works by Ibizan artists Antoni Marí Ribas Portmany and Rafel Tur i Costa, alongside the abstract art of Ibiza visitors Will Faber, Erwin Broner and Antoni Tàpies.

★ Top Tips

o Private vehicles (apart from residents') aren't allowed into Dalt Vila.

o Aside from the grand Portal de Ses Taules, there are three other entrances to this walled enclave, including the impressive Portal Nou (west side).

o The old town's steep, cobbled streets can be a challenge in flimsy sandals, flip-flops or high heels.

o Dalt Vila makes a spectacular location for dinner; you'll find good restaurants on Plaça de la Vila, Carrer de sa Carrossa and Plaça dels Desemparats.

✗ Take a Break

Boho cafe-bar S'Escalinata (p48) has low tables, cushioned seating and cool cocktails on a steep stone old-town staircase.

Downstairs, the archaeological site maps out Ibiza's history through the ages, from the Phoenicians to the Moorish era – contrasting beautifully with all the modern art around it.

Centre d'Interpretació Madina Yabisa

This tiny, fascinating Dalt Vila **interpretation centre** (Carrer Major 2; adult/child €2/free; ⏰10am-2pm & 6-9pm Tue-Fri Jul & Aug, 10am-2pm & 5-8pm Tue-Fri Apr-Jun & Sep, 10am-4.30pm Tue-Fri Oct-Mar, 10am-2pm Sat & Sun year-round) delves into the medieval Moorish city of Madina Yabisa (Ibiza Town), prior to the island's fall to Catalan forces in 1235. It's housed within the building that was, from the 15th century, the Casa de la Cúria (law courts). Parts

of the interior have been exposed to reveal the original Moorish-era defensive walls, including, interestingly, a Roman-era gravestone built into one corner. Artefacts, audiovisuals and maps transport visitors back in time.

Catedral

Ibiza's elegant **cathedral** (Plaça de la Catedral; ⏰9.30am-1.30pm & 4-8pm, hours vary), perched almost on Dalt Vila's highest point, combines several styles: the original 14th-century structure is Catalan Gothic, the sacristy was added in 1592 and a major baroque renovation took place in the 18th century. It was declared a cathedral in 1782 and now contains the **Museu Diocesà** (Plaça de la Catedral; admission €1.50; ⏰9.30am-1.30pm Tue-Sun,

Ibiza Town's Walls & Castle

Defensive Walls

Ibiza Town's towering defensive walls were constructed in the 16th century to safeguard local citizens from attacks by the Turkish navy and North African raiders. Ringing the entire Dalt Vila (p32) historic quarter, they were completed in 1585 and have been outstandingly preserved ever since.

The Carthaginians first built walls on Dalt Vila's high ground around the 5th century BC. These fortifications were later extended during the Moorish era – you can gain an excellent perspective on the town at this time, and see sections of the original Moorish walls, at the Centre d'Interpretació Madina Yabisa in Dalt Vila. Other walls from this period can be seen below the Baluard de Sant Jordi.

In the 16th century, after centuries of damage, Ibiza's crumbling defences were completely rebuilt and extended. Foreboding new fortifications were designed by Italian military engineer Giovanni Battista Calvi and architect Giacomo 'El Fratín', including the seven colossal *baluards* (bastions).

Today the walls of Dalt Vila – almost 2km long, 25m high and up to 5m thick – make up some of Europe's best-preserved fortifications, and form a key part of the city's Unesco World Heritage recognition.

Castell d'Eivissa

Occupying Dalt Vila's very highest ground, Ibiza's semiderelict **castle** (Ronda de l'Almudaina) is an assortment of historical buildings constructed over a 1000-year period, including the Moorish-era Tower of Homage, the former governor's residence, the 8th-century Almudaina (a Moorish keep) and, on the western side, infantry barracks from the 18th century. During the Spanish Civil War, mainland anarchists massacred over 100 Ibizan Nationalist prisoners here before fleeing the island.

Today, the castle's facade has been restored (after decades of neglect) and it is being transformed into a *parador* (luxurious state-owned hotel), which is expected to open in late 2022. The best view of the structure is from the huge bastion Baluard de Sant Bernat, on the southern side of Dalt Vila's ramparts, though the castle itself is closed to visitors.

closed Dec-Feb, hours vary), with impressive religious art spanning the 14th to 20th centuries. From the square outside, there are fantastic views of Dalt Vila and Ibiza's port.

Top Experience 📷

Soak Up the Summer Scene in the Port Area

Ibiza Town's Port Area has an immediate, addictive appeal. Wandering this atmospheric warren of tottering old fishermen's houses and cobbled streets, filled with uberchic boutiques and quirky market stalls, is an essential Ibiza experience. It isn't loaded with conventional sights: the fun is soaking up the summer scene and pure theatre of the Ibizan night from a harbourside terrace.

◎ MAP P44, F3

There's no public transport into the heart of the Port Area, but buses L10 and L15 stop on Avinguda de Santa Eulària, just west.

Passeig Marítim

Revamped in 2015, Ibiza Town's elegant **harbourside promenade** showcases the city's magnificent waterfront, and is lined with cafes, bars, boutiques, restaurants and market stalls. Yachts bob about on the marina on the north bank, while whitewashed old fishermen's homes cluster along its south side in the shadow of sparkling superyachts.

Mercat Vell

At the foot of Dalt Vila, Ibiza Town's graceful, columned neoclassical **Mercat Vell** (Old Market; Plaça de sa Constitució; ◷9am-9.30pm May-Oct, to 6pm Nov-Apr) has been the trading spot for island fruit and veg since 1872. Most of its produce, from olive oil and artisan bread to homemade quiches, is locally sourced, while the encircling cafes, bars and restaurants make the perfect perch for drinking in the action.

Carrer de la Verge

The slim 400m-long **Carrer de la Verge** (Carrer de la Mare de Déu; Sa Penya), running parallel to the harbour front, is named after the Virgin Mary, although these days it revolves around more bacchanalian pleasures than religious devotion. This is Ibiza's main LGBTIQ+ village, with around 20 bars, many of which are cave-like spaces that feel like they've been hacked out of the hillside.

During July and August the snug streetside terraces are packed with drinkers, and there's a heady ambience as the sultry Ibiza night is celebrated into the early hours.

Monument als Corsaris

Halfway along the Passeig Marítim stands this 1905 **stone obelisk** honouring Ibiza's corsairs – privateers licensed by the Spanish crown to

---

★ Top Tips

○ The Port Area is very quiet between November and Easter, with many bars closed.

○ Look for happy-hour deals at waterside bars and terraces.

○ Harbour-front bars charge much more for drinks than those just inland, including on Plaça des Parc.

○ The cafes on Plaça de sa Constitució enjoy fantastic views of the Portal de Ses Taules, leading up into Dalt Vila.

○ The dark lanes south of (above) Carrer de la Verge comprise a poor *barrio* (district) where street crime can occasionally be an issue. Take care after dark.

✕ Take a Break

Comidas Bar San Juan (p48) offers excellent-value, no-nonsense Spanish cuisine served at shared tables.

Alternatively, pull up a marketside chair and tuck into a deliciously fresh juice or something stronger at laid-back cafe Croissant Show (p50).

combat the threat of North African raiders, as well as the British and the French. The monument faces a small square, Plaça d'Antoni Riquer, named after the legendary Ibizan corsair responsible for capturing the major British ship, *Felicity*, in 1806.

Vara de Rey Monument

Ibiza Town's **Vara de Rey Monument** (Passeig de Vara de Rey; pictured) depicts the Ibizan general Joachim Vara de Rey, who died in the 1898 Battle of El Caney, fought between Spain and the USA over Cuba. It's on Ibiza's most beautiful boulevard, which is traffic-free, dotted with cafes and graced by elegant town houses.

Moorish Ibiza

The Arrival of the Moors

The Moors made irregular raids on Ibiza and the Balearics in the 8th and 9th centuries AD, but they did not take formal control until 902, when the Emir of Córdoba launched an invasion of the islands. At the time, Ibiza was a poor, isolated backwater, with minimal links to the outside world. Moorish rule brought many benefits in both tolerance and prosperity; above all it introduced specialised hydraulic-engineering systems that transformed the agricultural and salt-production sectors, enabling crops such as rice and sugar cane to be grown.

A Booming City

Ibiza Town thrived under Moorish rule, becoming a prosperous port with bustling markets. The city gained a new name (Yabisa), language (Arabic) and religion (Islam). Yabisa was divided into three areas, with the fortified castle and palace at the top, a middle residential and market zone, and a lower section bordering the port. Most of Ibiza Town's port-level defensive walls were established during the Moorish period. The excellent Centre d'Interpretació Madina Yabisa (p34) is highly illuminating about the city's Moorish era.

The Fall of Moorish Ibiza

For 200 years, under tolerant *walis* (governors), Yabisa was a stable, flourishing city. Away from it, ancient ways survived in rural areas, where Christianity was often practised. Trouble erupted from 1085 onwards, when control of the Balearics passed to the Al-Murtada dynasty, which raided towns in mainland Spain and Italy from the islands. In 1114 thousands of Pisan and Catalan troops, backed by the pope, formed a mini-crusade and invaded Ibiza. Although Christian forces laid siege to Yabisa, massacring the Moorish population, demolishing the city's walls and ending Al-Murtada rule, they didn't take control. The Moorish Almoravid dynasty took power, only to be ousted by the Moorish Almohads in 1188.

Moorish rule came to a definitive end when Catalan forces took Yabisa on 8 August 1235 after a long siege. Mallorca had been conquered by the Spanish Christians in 1229; Menorca followed in 1287. Catalan replaced Arabic as Ibiza's main language, Catholicism became the official religion and Yabisa was renamed Eivissa.

Top Experience 📷

Bask on the Beaches of Botafoc & Talamanca

The upmarket Botafoc area, on the north side of Ibiza's harbour, contains luxury apartment blocks, a casino, a yacht club and marina, and the clubs Pacha (p52), Lío (p53) and Heart (p53). There's a sprinkling of cafes and restaurants with fine Dalt Vila views. Just north of Botafoc is Talamanca, a half-moon bay with golden sands, safe swimming, and several hotels and restaurants.

◉ MAP P44, G2

Walk 30 minutes from Ibiza Town to Marina Botafoc.

Bus L12B from Ibiza Town (€1.65, hourly).

Boat Year-round from Passeig Marítim (€2.60, every 10 to 30 minutes), with Barcas de Talamanca.

Platja de Talamanca

This sheltered, sandy bay, 3km east of Ibiza Town, is the best **beach** within walking distance of the capital. Tourism development hasn't been too unkind to Talamanca, and there's good family-friendly swimming thanks to calm, shallow waters, plus several excellent seaside restaurants ranging from simple *chiringuitos* (beach bars) to glossy hotel eateries.

Botafoc Marina

Encompassing the northern part of Ibiza Town's harbour, the **marina** is one of Europe's most exclusive. Gleaming yachts bob beside fancy cafes and restaurants and a clutch of major clubs.

Ses Feixes

Just inland from Talamanca beach, the scruffy-looking **Ses Feixes** (admission free) marshlands and fields of reeds and scrub were once Ibiza Town's vegetable garden. They were developed by the Moors over 1000 years ago, using innovative water management and crop rotation to produce two crops a year. Though cultivated until the 1950s, the area is now a haven for birdlife, including herons. On a wander through, you'll spot the arched, ancient *portals de feixa*, marking the entrance to each individual plot.

Botafoc Peninsula

East of the Botafoc marina, the narrow Botafoc peninsula is the site of Ibiza's main ferry terminal. A **lighthouse** marks its easternmost point.

★ Top Tips

o Talamanca beach is sheltered and shallow, so it's ideal for kids who aren't strong swimmers.

o On summer weekends, Talamanca gets packed with families from Ibiza Town. You may want to hunt down a more secluded strand further out of town.

o Talamanca beach is just a couple of kilometres south of the village of Jesús, home to a handsome 15th-century church (p48).

✗ Take a Break

With its affordable prices, uncomplicated menu and shoreside setting, Bar Flotante (p51) is an excellent Talamanca venue for seafood, omelettes, *bocadillos* (filled rolls) or just a beer with a view.

Glitz meals up at the **Nobu Hotel Ibiza Bay** (www.nobuhotelibizabay.com; Camí Ses Feixes 52), where it's a choice between upmarket Mexican, Japanese and Mediterranean restaurants and a gluten-free bakery.

Ibiza Town & Around Bask on the Beaches of Botafoc & Talamanca

Walking Tour 🚶

Nightcrawlers' Ibiza Town

The port is by far Ibiza's most atmospheric area for an evening out. Kick off on intimate Plaça des Parc, before heading east along the view-laden harbour for drinks on one of its many terraces (keep an eye out for happy-hour deals). Then head back along LGBTIQ+-friendly Carrer de la Verge to Carrer d'Alfons XII, where club parades often terminate.

Walk Facts

Start Plaça des Parc
Finish Carrer d'Alfons XII
Length 1km

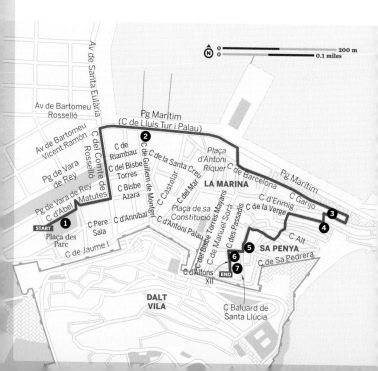

❶ Madagascar

A popular choice on traffic-free Plaça des Parc, cheerful cafe-bar **Madagascar** (📞971 30 73 98; Plaça des Parc; 🕙9am-2am May-Sep, to 11.45pm Oct-Apr; 🛜) is great for fuelling up on fresh juices, *bocadillos* or tapas before the night ahead. In the evening, it's a relaxed bar, with well-priced *combinados* (spirits with mixer) and draught beer.

❷ Can Pou

Claiming to be Ibiza's oldest cafe, this atmospheric **bar** (p53) has a great terrace facing the harbour.

❸ The Rock

Towards the promenade's eastern end, **The Rock** (Carrer Garijo 14; 🕙11pm-4am May-Oct) is a meeting point for club promoters and dance-music-industry types, so it's a good bet for finding out what's on and bumping into a DJ or two. It has a fab harbour-front terrace, and all club parades pass here at some stage in the night.

❹ Sunrise

One of the most popular bars on LGBTIQ+-oriented 'Street of the Virgin', **Sunrise** (📞677 489827; www.facebook.com/sunriseibiza; Carrer de la Verge 44; 🕙10pm-4am Apr-Nov) has a gorgeous interior, with a disco ball and swings dangling by the bar. It's friendly and welcoming, with a decadent cocktail list, occasional live DJs and some of the strip's most packed-out tables.

❺ Bar 1805

Tucked away on a Sa Penya backstreet terrace, boho **Bar 1805** (📞651 625972; www.bar1805ibiza.com; Carrer Baluard de Santa Llúcia 7; 🕙8pm-4am mid-Apr–Oct; 🛜) mixes some of the town's best cocktails, with lots of absinthe action on its beautifully illustrated menu. Try the signature Green Beast (served in a punchbowl) or a Gin-Basil Smash, which arrives in a teacup.

❻ Soap at Dome

A famous gay bar known as the final destination for Ibiza's night-defining club parades. Around midnight in summer, the **Soap at Dome** (📞971 19 39 31; www.facebook.com/soapatdomeibiza; Carrer d'Alfons XII 5; 🕙11pm-3am Easter–mid-Oct) terrace is full-on theatre, with costumes galore and a joyous buzz in the air. Expect the unexpected, as gold-paint-sprayed dancers, bondage queens and leather kings, bearing club banners and dispensing promo flyers, jostle for attention. Business hours may have changed due to the pandemic; call ahead before visiting.

❼ Angelo

Hugging the city walls, **Angelo** (www.facebook.com/barangeloibiza; Carrer d'Alfons XII 11; 🕙7pm-4am May-Oct) is a busy LGBTIQ+ bar with several levels and a popular international rooftop restaurant. The atmosphere is relaxed and the crowd mixed. Nearby are a handful of other LGBTIQ+-oriented bars.

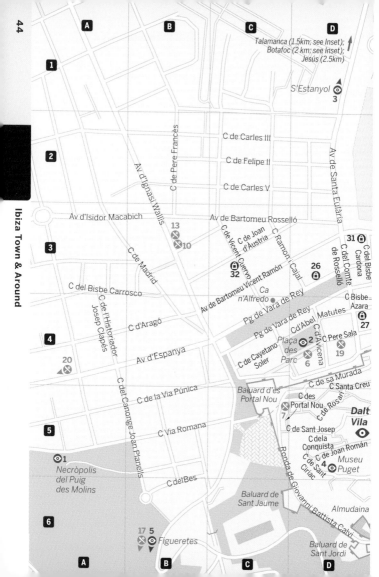

Talamanca (1.5km; see Inset);
Botafoc (2 km; see Inset);
Jesús (2.5km)

S'Estanyol ⊚ 3

C de Carles III

C de Felipe II

C de Carles V

Av d'Ignasi Wallis

C de Pere Francès

Av de Santa Eulària

Av d'Isidor Macabich

Av de Bartomeu Rosselló

13 ⊗
⊗ 10

C de Madrid

C de Vicent Cuervo

C de Joan d'Àustria

C Ramon i Cajal

C del Comte de Rosselló

31 ⓐ
C del Bisbe Cardona

🔒 32

26 ⓐ

C Bisbe Azara

ⓐ 27

C del Bisbe Carrosco

Av de Bartomeu Vicent Ramón

Ca n'Alfredo ●

C de l'Historiador Josep Clapés

C d'Aragó

Pg de Vara de Rey

Pg de Vara de Rey

Cd'Abel Matutes

C d'Avicena

C Pere Sala
⊗ 19

Av d'Espanya

Plaça des Parc ⊚ 2
6

C de Cayetano Soler

20 ◀⊗

C de la Via Púnica

C del Canonge Joan Planells

C Via Romana

Baluard d'es Portal Nou

⊗ C des Portal Nou
7 ↙

C de sa Murada

C Santa Creu
C de Rosar

Dalt Vila
⊚

C de Sant Josep
C dela Conquista
C de Joan Román

Museu ● Puget
4 ⊚

C de Sant Ciriac

⊚ 1
Necròpolis del Puig des Molins

C del Bes

Ronda de Giovanni Battista Calvi

Baluard de Sant Jaume

Almudaina

17 5
⊗ ⊚ Figueretes

Baluard de Sant Jordi

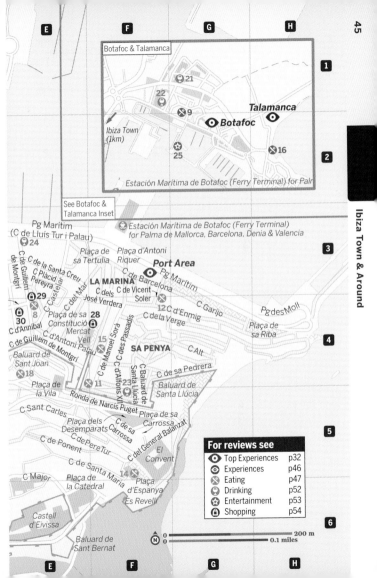

E **F** **G** **H**

Botafoc & Talamanca

1

21

22

9

25

16

Talamanca

Botafoc

Ibiza Town
(1km)

2

Estación Marítima de Botafoc (Ferry Terminal) for Palm

See Botafoc &
Talamanca Inset

Estación Marítima de Botafoc (Ferry Terminal)
for Palma de Mallorca, Barcelona, Denia & Valencia

3

Pg Marítim
(C de Lluís Tur i Palau)
24

Plaça de
sa Tertulia

Plaça d'Antoni
Riquer

Port Area

C de la Santa Creu
C Plàcid
Pereyra

C del Mar
C dels
José Verdera

C de Vicent
Soler

LA MARINA

C de Barcelona

Pg Marítim

C Garijo

Pgdes Moll

C de Guillem de Montgrí

29

C d'Enmig

12

C de la Verge

Plaça de
sa Riba

4

8

30

Plaça de sa
Constitució

Mercat
Vell

C d'Antoni Palau

15

28

C de Manuel Sorà

C des Passadis

C d'Alfons XII

SA PENYA

C Alt

C d'Annibal
C de Guillem de Montgrí

Baluard de
Sant Joan

18

11

C de sa Pedrera

23

C Baluard de
Santa Llúcia

Baluard de
Santa Llúcia

Plaça de
la Vila

Ronda de Narcís Puget

C de sa
Carrossa

Plaça de sa
Carrossa

5

C Sant Carles

Plaça dels
Desemparats

C de Pere Tur

C de Ponent

C del General Balanzat

El
Convent

C Major

Plaça de
Santa Maria

14

Plaça de
la Catedral

Plaça
d'Espanya

Es Revell

**Castell
d'Eivissa**

Baluard de
Sant Bernat

N
0   200 m
0   0.1 miles

6

E **F** **G** **H**

Ibiza Town & Around

For reviews see	
⊙ Top Experiences	p32
⊙ Experiences	p46
⊗ Eating	p47
⊖ Drinking	p52
☆ Entertainment	p53
⌂ Shopping	p54

Experiences

Necròpolis del Puig des Molins
HISTORIC SITE

1 MAP P44, A5

Today it looks like little more than rocky scrubland, but this vast ancient burial ground was a key part of Ibiza Town's 1999 World Heritage recognition. The earliest tombs date from the 7th century BC and Phoenician times. The museum displays finds (amulets, jewellery, vases, terracotta figurines) from the more than 3000 tombs that honeycomb the hillside. Outside, peer into the *hypogea* (burial caverns) cut deep into the hill; you can descend into an interlocking series of these.

It's thought that Ibiza became an A-list cemetery for wealthy Carthaginians because their burial requirements were very specific – among them was the need for a location free from poisonous creatures, and there are no snakes or scorpions on the island. Nobles were buried in this necropolis in their thousands, with their bodies transported here from all over the empire. (Carrer Via Romana 31; adult/child €2.40/free; ☉10am-2pm & 6.30-9pm Tue-Sat Apr-Sep, 9.30am-3pm Tue-Sat Oct-Mar, 10am-2pm Sun year-round)

Plaça des Parc
SQUARE

2 MAP P44, D4

Revamped in 2017, this pretty, traffic-free square is the bohemian heart of Ibiza Town, fringed by cafe-bars, restaurants and boutiques. Grab a table and take it all in as club promoters discuss DJ line-ups, shoppers take a breather and clubbers grumble about comedowns.

S'Estanyol
BEACH

3 MAP P44, D1

Something of a secret beach, S'Estanyol is a tiny, gorgeous pebbly cove, only accessible by a dirt road (rough in parts). A few fishing huts dot the seaweed-filled shoreline and offshore you'll find excellent snorkelling. It's 3km northeast of Talamanca, signposted from the northeast end of the bay; the last 1.5km is a dirt track.

By the shore, boho-cool *chiringuito* **Cala Bonita** (☎605 450592, 971 94 86 21; http://calabonita ibiza.com; mains €14-25; ☉1-9pm Mar-Jan) serves fresh seafood, paella, contemporary tapas and a smart, local-produce-infused Mediterranean menu to a background of quality DJ beats.

Museu Puget
GALLERY

4 MAP P44, D5

A 15th-century mansion, with a typical late-Gothic courtyard and staircase, houses 130 paintings by Ibizan artist Narcís Puget Viñas (1874–1960) and his son, Narcís Puget Riquer (1916–83), both focused on capturing the colours of local life on the island.

(www.eivissa.es/mace; Carrer Major 18; admission free; 10am-2pm & 6-9pm Tue-Fri Jul & Aug, 10am-2pm & 5-8pm Tue-Fri Apr-Jun & Sep, 10am-4.30pm Tue-Fri Oct-Mar, 10am-2pm Sat & Sun year-round)

Figueretes BEACH

5 ⊙ MAP P44, B6

Southwest of Dalt Vila, the slender bay of the Figueretes neighbourhood is the closest patch of sand to Ibiza Town, with a palm-lined promenade and several sea-facing restaurants. It's 1km southwest of central Ibiza Town – about a 15-minute walk.

Eating

Locals Only MEDITERRANEAN €€

6 ✖ MAP P44, D4

On buzzy Plaça des Parc, organic-focused Locals Only gets much-deserved rave reviews for its excellent contemporary Mediterranean-Italian food, at sensible prices. Pick between the bubbly terrace and stylish interior, then tuck into inventive salads, perfect pastas or any of the daily specials chalked on a board. House wines are well selected (and priced), and staff are professional and informed. (971 30 19 97; www.localsonlyibiza. com; Plaça des Parc 5; mains €10-20; noon-1.30am Mar–mid-Dec, closed Mon Mar-May & Oct–mid-Dec;)

Necròpolis del Puig des Molins

KAROL KOZLOWSKI/SHUTTERSTOCK ©

Ibiza Town & Around Eating

S'Escalinata
MEDITERRANEAN €

7 ✖ MAP P44, C5

With its low-slung tables and colourful cushions cascading down a steep stone staircase, this boho-chic cafe-bar-restaurant enjoys a magical location inside Dalt Vila. On the tempting menu are healthy breakfasts, tapas, *bocadillos* and delicious light dinners of hummus, tortilla or goat's-cheese salads. It's open late into the night, mixing up freshly squeezed juices, G&Ts and fruity cocktails. (☏ 653 371356; Carrer des Portal Nou 10; dishes €7-13; ◷ 10am-3am Apr-Oct; 🛜)

Comidas Bar San Juan
SPANISH €

8 ✖ MAP P44, E4

More traditional than trendy, this popular family-run operation, with two small dining rooms, harks back to the days before Ibiza be-

---

Església de Jesús

Just 2km north of Talamanca beach, the bustling village of **Jesús** is home to a beautiful whitewashed church dating back to 1466, with a pillared portico added at the turn of the 20th century. It's particularly notable for its extraordinary Gothic altarpiece – its central face of the Virgin is considered a masterpiece of Balearic medieval iconography.

---

came a byword for glam. It offers outstanding value, with fish dishes and steaks for around €10, plus omelettes, salads, croquettes, cheese platters and other local favourites. No reservations, so arrive early and expect to share your table. (☏ 971 31 16 03; Carrer de Guillem de Montgrí 8; mains €7-11; ◷ 1-3.30pm & 8.30-11pm Mon-Sat)

Passion
HEALTH FOOD €€

9 ✖ MAP P44, G2

Part of Lana Love's healthy-eating Ibiza empire, with views across the marina to Dalt Vila, this stylish cafe deals in divine organic, vegetarian and vegan bites. Dangling lanterns, communal tables and a semi-open terrace create a boho setting for elegantly prepped breakfasts, from smashed avocado and scrambled eggs to fruit-sprinkled granola and fresh smoothies. Good for lunch (pastas, salads), too.

Branches also in Santa Eulària (p89) and Platja d'en Bossa (p76). (☏ 971 31 45 66; http://passion-ibiza. com; Passeig Joan Carles I 23, Edificio Mediterráneo, Marina Ibiza; breakfasts €6.50-15, mains €9-16; ◷ 9.30am-midnight May-Oct, to 4pm Nov-Apr)

Can Terra
PINTXOS, TAPAS €€

10 ✖ MAP P44, B3

A stylish tapas bar, with a sandstone-walled interior and lovely back patio, which is rammed most nights with *ibicencos* devouring delectable tapas and dishes such as *sepia a la plancha* (grilled cuttlefish), and sipping *cañas* (small draught beers) and Spanish wines. Be prepared to wait for a table. Also great for breakfasts of *tostadas* (toasted baguette), *pinchos de tortilla* and fresh orange juice. (📞971 31 00 64; http://canterraibiza.com; Avinguda d'Ignasi Wallis 14; tapas €3, mains €9-16; ⏰8.30am-2am)

La Bodega   TAPAS, INTERNATIONAL €€

11 MAP P44, E4

In the shadow of Dalt Vila's walls, packed-out La Bodega serves up subtly contemporary Spanish-international tapas in a stylishly converted storehouse with open-stone walls, vaulted ceilings and tiled floors. Sharing platters wander from chickpea salad, spinach quiche and ceramic bowls of hummus to classic *tortilla de patatas* (potato omelette), and you'll uncover some alluring Ibizan wines. It's popular; reserve ahead. (📞971 19 27 40; www.labodegaibiza.es; Carrer del Bisbe Torres Mayans 2; tapas €4-10, raciones €7-15; ⏰6pm-2am Apr–mid-Oct)

Los Pasajeros   SPANISH €€

12 MAP P44, F4

Between club-night posters, pounding house music, shared bench-style tables and a fun young vibe, Los Pasajeros plates up gigantic portions of hearty, uncomplicated Spanish favourites, including *gambas al ajillo* (prawns in garlic and oil), pork sirloin in honey-mustard sauce, and melted cheese with fig jam. Service is efficient, there's *tinto de verano* (similar to sangria) by the

Ca n'Alfredo

Locals have been flocking to family-run **Ca n'Alfredo's** (Map p44; 📞971 31 12 74; www.canalfredo.com; Passeig de Vara de Rey 16; mains €20-30; ⏰1-5pm & 8pm-1am Tue-Sat, 1-5pm Sun) on leafy Vara de Rey since 1934. It's a great place for the freshest of seafood and other classic Ibizan dishes that are so good it's essential to book. Try John Dory fillets in almond sauce, or a traditional dish from the dedicated Ibizan cuisine menu, all accompanied by an impressive selection of Balearic wines.

litre (€10) and prices are as pleasingly down-to-earth as the cooking.

It's hidden up a narrow staircase, where everyone crams in to queue. (📞653 350961; manime82@hotmail.com; Carrer de Vicent Soler 6; mains €10-15; ⏰1-4pm & 7.30pm-midnight Mon-Fri, 7pm-midnight Sat)

Mar a Vila   PINTXOS, TAPAS €€

13 MAP P44, B3

Sweet, relaxed tapas specialist Mar a Vila brings a splash of the sea to city-centre Ibiza and conceals a pretty courtyard. The tapas and *pintxos* (Basque tapas; €1.50), stacked on the bar, are bang on the money (try the red pepper stuffed with goat's cheese), as are deliciously contemporary mains such as pork

STBAUS7/GETTY IMAGES ©

La Torreta

ribs with Ibizan herbs or pumpkin-and-asparagus risotto. (📞971 31 47 78; www.facebook.com/maravilaibiza; Avinguda d'Ignasi Wallis 16; mains €9-14; ⏱8.45am-1am Mon-Fri, 11am-1am Sat Feb–mid-Dec)

Hotel Mirador de Dalt Vila
MEDITERRANEAN €€€

14 ✖ MAP P44, F5

You'll dine magnificently at this intimate restaurant, with its painted barrel ceiling and original canvases, in a grand, dusty-pink 20th-century house. Service is discreet yet friendly, delivering creative, colourful and delightfully presented gourmet Mediterranean dishes such as duck cannelloni and red-shrimp rice with cuttlefish. Grab cocktails in the cosy bar, which has an underfloor display of antiquities from the sea. Book ahead. (📞971 30 30 45; www.hotelmiradoribiza.com; Plaça d'Espanya 4; mains €40, degustation menu €100; ⏱1-4pm & 8pm-midnight Easter-Oct; 🛜)

Croissant Show
CAFE €

15 ✖ MAP P44, F4

Opposite Ibiza Town's local-produce market, this low-key cafe is where everyone pops in for an impressive range of pastries and post-partying breakfast goodies, along with salads, pastas, quiches, crepes and sandwiches. Grab a table on the people-watching terrace and a freshly squeezed juice mixed with fruit straight from the market. Cash only. (📞971 31 76 65;

www.facebook.com/croissant.show.5; Plaça de sa Constitució 2; tapas €2, dishes €5-14; ⏲6am-midnight; 🔊)

Bar Flotante
SPANISH €€

16 ⊗ MAP P44, G2

Offering tables so close to the sea that you can almost dip your toes in the Mediterranean over lunch, this laid-back, moderately priced bar-restaurant at the southwest end of Talamanca beach is always popular. There are grilled meats, fresh fish, omelettes, salads, *boca-dillos* and good house wines. (📞971 19 04 66; Platja de Talamanca; dishes €7.50-20; ⏲9am-11.30pm Feb-Nov)

Soleado
FRENCH €€

17 ⊗ MAP P44, B6

Figueretes' seafront promenade has a stack of mediocre restaurants, but friendly Soleado is a cut above most. The menu is Provençal, with fine seafood, meat and fish (such as grilled sea bream with chorizo). There's a lovely terrace jutting out above the beach, along with a €24 three-course set menu. Figueretes is a 1km, 15-minute walk southwest of the centre. (📞971 39 48 11; www.soleadoibiza.com; Passeig de ses Pitiuses, Figueretes; mains €18-24; ⏲6.30pm-midnight Thu-Tue mid-Apr–mid-Oct)

La Torreta
MEDITERRANEAN €€€

18 ⊗ MAP P44, E4

Huddled on a lively old-town square, La Torreta offers some of Dalt Vila's best cuisine, par-ticularly its delicately prepared seafood, pastas and desserts. Eat on the buzzing front terrace or, for that special Ibiza setting, book the dining room that occupies one of Dalt Vila's medieval defence towers. Service is excellent, though it does get very busy; reserve ahead. (📞971 30 04 11; Plaça de la Vila 10; mains €17-29; ⏲7pm-1am May-Oct)

La Brasa
MEDITERRANEAN €€€

19 ⊗ MAP P44, D4

La Brasa is as popular for its quality fish and meat, sizzled over charcoal, as for its paellas and Mediterranean dishes crafted with ingredients from its own organic garden. Try savoury delights such as courgette-flower tempura or entrecôte in green-pepper sauce, served on a romantic fairy-lit terrace shaded by vines, palms, banana trees and bursts of bougainvillea.

Fish Shack

Perched sea-side on the far east tip of Talamanca bay, **Fish Shack** (Platja de Talamanca; mains €13-23; ⏲11am-midnight May-Oct) is a no-nonsense *chiringuito* and one of the most popular in-the-know seafood spots on the island. The thing is the deliciously fresh daily-caught fish, served grilled with potatoes and salad. Cards aren't accepted. Bookings can only be made in person and require a minimum of seven people.

Perhaps best visited outside high season (when the kitchen and service can struggle). (☏971 30 12 02; www.labrasaibiza.com; Carrer Pere Sala 3; mains €18-32; ⊙noon-late)

Bar 43 Tapas TAPAS €€

20 ✖ MAP P44, A4

A cosy, down-to-earth bar that distinguishes itself with its warm welcome and generously portioned tapas – *gambas al ajillo*, *boquerones* (marinated ancho-vies), *tortilla de patatas*, spinach croquettes and the like. Go for the good buzz and reasonable prices. (☏971 30 09 92; www.ibiza-43.com; Avinguda d'Espanya 43; raciones €4.50-12; ⊙8pm-2am Mon-Sat; 🛜)

Drinking

Pacha CLUB

21 🍸 MAP P44, G1

Going strong since 1973, Pacha is Ibiza's original megaclub and the islanders' party venue of choice. It's built around the shell of a farm-house, boasting a multilevel main dance floor, a Funky Room (for soul and disco beats), a huge VIP section and myriad other places to dance or lounge.

These include a fabulous open-air terrace, a Global Room for hip-hop and R&B, and the Sweet Pacha area for '80s and '90s hits. Virtu-ally anyone who's anyone in the DJ world has spun the decks here, including the likes of Paul Oaken-fold, Sasha and Roger Sanchez.

Can Pou

JOTAPG/SHUTTERSTOCK ©

There are now Pacha clubs all over the world, and the brand has established a global reputation for chic Balearic-style clubbing. (www.pachaibiza.com; Avinguda 8 d'Agost; from €15; ⊘midnight-7am May-Sep)

Heart

CLUB

22 🚇 MAP P44, F2

A fabulous collaboration between Canadian Cirque du Soleil founder Guy Laliberté and Catalan star chefs Ferran and Albert Adrià, Heart is a creative, high-end fusion of performance art, live bands, electronic club nights and elaborate cuisine. Book in advance for dance-theatre shows over imaginative Adrià-designed dinners (minimum spend €215 per person), or come for Ibiza's famous gay-friendly La Troya Wednesdays, which relocated here in 2017. (☏971 93 37 77; www.heartibiza.com; Passeig Joan Carles I 17, Marina Ibiza; admission €20; ⊘from 9pm May-Oct)

Lola's

CLUB

23 🚇 MAP P44, F5

Having returned with a bang in 2016, this gay-Ibiza legend is now the island's only exclusively gay party-all-night dance club. Pack into the small underground interior, which gets busy around 3.30am when all the other bars close, or swing by for the weekly electronic Frigay events (on, yes, Fridays). (www.facebook.com/lolas.ibiza.disco; Carrer d'Alfons XII 9; admission incl drink €10-15; ⊘midnight-6.30am daily May-Oct, Thu-Sat Nov-Apr)

Clubbing Outside Ibiza Town

Just 6km northeast of Ibiza Town, the inland village of **Sant Rafel** hosts two of the world's most renowned superclubs. **Amnesia** (p57) is legendary: this is where the Balearic Beat (a mix of acid house, indie, funk and disco) music explosion kicked off in the late 1980s. Over the road is **Privilege** (p57), the world's largest club, which hosted Ibiza's wild, world-famous Manumission nights for more than a decade between 1994 and 2006.

Can Pou

BAR, CAFE

24 🚇 MAP P44, E3

This harbour-front bar attracts a loyal local crowd thanks to its fairly moderate prices (wines €3.50, *combinados* €8.50) and its claim to be Ibiza's oldest cafe. The interior is atmospheric (the building is centuries old), but the great marina-facing terrace is the real appeal. Tapas are served and there's occasional live music. (☏971 31 08 75; www.facebook.com/canpouibiza; Carrer Lluís Tur i Palau 19; ⊘8am-4am mid-Apr–mid-Oct; 🛜)

Entertainment

Lío

CABARET, LIVE MUSIC

25 ⭐ MAP P44, G2

Basking in perfect views of Dalt Vila from its terrace, this multifaceted Pacha-group venue arguably enjoys the best location in Ibiza. It's aimed at an older crowd, featuring gourmet dining, cabaret shows and live music. Expect to shell out some serious cash (upwards of €120) and reserve ahead; dinner bookings include all entertainment. After 1am it morphs into a club. (☎971 31 00 22; https://lioibiza.com; Passeig Joan Carles I, Marina Ibiza; ⏰7pm-6am May-Sep)

Shopping

Charo Ruiz
FASHION & ACCESSORIES

26 🅰 MAP P44, D3

Step into the fashion-forward world of Ibiza-based, Seville-born designer Charo Ruiz, famous for her elegant, figure-hugging, island-inspired women's couture creations – originally flogged at local markets. Her collections of skimpy crop-tops, slinky dresses and breezy kaftans have a boho-chic, beach-glam feel, featuring beautiful embroidery and crochet-work, statement colours and Adlib flair. (☎971 19 23 35; www.charoruiz.com; Passeig de Vara de Rey 4; ⏰11am-10pm)

Sombrerería Bonet
HATS

27 🅰 MAP P44, D4

Going strong since 1916, this celebrated hat specialist sells an enticing selection of headgear, including panamas, trilbies, berets and cowboy hats in traditional styles (and also contemporary colours), mostly in the €15 to €60 range. Woven Ibizan bags and baskets from natural fibres are also stocked. (☎971 31 06 68; Carrer del Comte de Rosselló 6; ⏰10am-2pm & 5-8pm Mon-Sat)

Babaz
FASHION & ACCESSORIES

28 🅰 MAP P44, F4

This glitzy boutique on Ibiza Town's market square is lined with boho-luxe fashion creations from much-loved French label Antik Batik, which specialises in gorgeous kaftans, breezy dresses, bold prints and glittery sandals. There are also stylish bags, jewellery, shoes, shawls and more. (☎971 31 57 06; http://babazibiza.com; Plaça de sa Constitució 8; ⏰11am-midnight Apr-Oct & mid-Dec–mid-Jan)

Ibiza Bagús
FASHION & ACCESSORIES

29 🅰 MAP P44, E3

Sparkly sequins, jazzy pom-poms, floaty fabrics and rainbows of summer-inspired neon colours set a fun tone for kaftans, dresses, sandals, bags and plenty more women's style at this boho-Ibiza boutique in the thick of Ibiza Town. Three other branches are scattered around nearby, and prices are perfectly reasonable (by Ibiza standards!). (☎971 19 13 13; http://ibizabagus.es; Carrer de Guillem de Montgrí 12; ⏰11am-11.30pm)

reVOLVER
FASHION & ACCESSORIES

30 🅰 MAP P44, E4

Known for its carefully curated couture collections, reVOLVER is all about subtly luxurious dresses, shirts, jeans and shoes from the likes of Kenzo, Alexander McQueen and Sass & Bide. Expect bold looks and plenty of black in the stripped-back yet flashy, contemporary boutique. Designer sunglasses, from Linda Farrow to Victoria Beckham, are its other speciality. (☏ 971 31 89 39; www.revolveribiza.com; Carrer Bisbe Azara 1; ⊙ 10.30am-2pm & 5-11pm Mon-Sat year-round, plus 6-9pm Sun Jun-Sep)

Pacha
FASHION & ACCESSORIES

31 🏠 MAP P44, D3

There are Pacha stores across the island (and beyond), but you can't beat shopping a stone's throw from this global superclub's HQ. Stocks bags, accessories, mixed CDs and clothing for men,

women and kids. (www.pacha collection.com; Carrer de Lluís Tur i Palau 20; ⊙ 10am-2.30am May–mid-Sep, 10am-2pm & 5-8pm mid-Sep–Jan & Easter)

Campos de Ibiza
PERFUME, COSMETICS

32 🏠 MAP P44, C3

Focused on perfumes infused with summery island scents (such as mandarin, jasmine or almond blossom), Campos de Ibiza is a fab little spot for picking up a piece of Ibiza to take home with you. Lovely scented candles, moisturisers and bath salts, too. (☏ 971 93 42 89; http://camposdeibiza.com; Carrer de Vicent Cuervo 13; ⊙ 10.30am-9.30pm Mon-Sat, to 1.30pm Sun Apr-Oct, 10.30am-1.30pm & 5-8.30pm Mon-Sat Nov-Mar)

Pacha

Top Experience 📸
Dance the Night Away in Sant Rafel de Sa Creu

Close to the island's centre, the small village of Sant Rafel is equidistant from the raunchy bar action of Sant Antoni and the classy nightlife, historical riches and cosmopolitan culture of Ibiza Town. Its two blockbuster attractions are megaclubs, Amnesia and Privilege, but if you've no interest in dance-floor action, Sant Rafel also has good restaurants and a lovely church.

Bus L3 (every 15 to 60 minutes) runs to/from Ibiza Town and Sant Antoni.

The Discobus shuttles clubbers to/from Amnesia and Privilege.

Amnesia

Amnesia (📞 971 19 80 41; www.amnesia.es; Carretera Eivissa-Sant Antoni Km 5, Sant Rafel de Sa Creu; €40-70; 🕐midnight-6am late May-Oct) is arguably Ibiza's most influential and legendary club, its decks welcoming such DJ royalty as Sven Väth, Paul Van Dyk, Paul Oakenfold, Tiësto and Avicii. There's a warehouse-like main room and a terrace topped by a graceful atrium. Big nights include techno-fests Cocoon and Music On, trance-mad Cream and foam-filled Espuma, which always draws a big local crowd.

Amnesia's origins actually go back to the 18th century, when the farmhouse the club has been built around was first constructed. It was a venue for hippy gatherings in the 1970s, then became Ibiza's first after-hours club in the mid-1980s with Balearic tunes played in the sunshine by the legendary DJ Alfredo. Amnesia's underground, innovative musical policy made it the most fashionable club on the island.

Privilege

The world's biggest club, **Privilege** (www.privilegeibiza.com; Carretera Eivissa-Sant Antoni, Sant Rafel de Sa Creu; €35-60; 🕐midnight-6am May-Sep) is a mind-blowing space that regularly hosts 10,000 clubbers. The venue was originally an open-air affair called Ku: stars including Freddie Mercury and James Brown headlined. Privilege's best times were undoubtedly during Manumission's (p59) infamous residency (1994–2006), with ground-breaking theatrics (including live sex shows). DJs Tiësto and Armin van Buuren have also enjoyed seasons here.

The main dance floor is an enormous, pulsating area, where the DJ's cabin is suspended above the crowd. VIP zones are located on upper levels, while an open-air dome forms a chill-out zone. Pick your night carefully; sometimes this vast venue can feel achingly empty. In the Coco Loco room, DJs spin alternative

★ Top Tips

○ There are ATMs in Sant Rafel centre.

○ You'll find several ceramic workshops and pottery shops in the village.

○ If you're clubbing, don't run across the busy Ibiza Town–Sant Rafel highway; deaths have occurred here. Use the bridges.

○ Drinks (even water) in the two mega-clubs are ludicrously expensive.

✕ Take a Break

On Sant Rafel's main street, **Ca'n Pilot** (📞 971 19 82 93; http://asadorcanpilot.com; Carretera Eivissa-Sant Antoni; mains €12-21; 🕐noon-4pm & 8-11pm Thu-Tue) is a busy spot for Spanish-style grilled meats, with excellent lamb, *pollo payés* (country chicken) and beef. Order the *chuletón* (T-bone steak) for two and they'll bring a small grill to the table, so you finish cooking it yourself to personal taste. Book ahead in summer.

sounds, and in the back room there are sometimes live acts.

Església de Sant Rafel

Built in the late 18th century, Sant Rafel's typically Ibizan **church** (Plaça Joan Marí Cardona; ⊙dawn-dusk, hours vary) is perched on a hilltop 300m southeast of the village's main street, surrounded by palms and flowers. Its whitewashed facade and walls make it a local landmark, particularly when floodlit at night. Fronting the church is a pretty little square with fine views down to Dalt Vila.

Dining Out

Little Sant Rafel hosts a handful of eateries, ranging from glitzy boho-style garden restaurants to good old simple Spanish grills. Arrive early or book ahead in summer.

Nearby: Casita Verde

Established in 1996, this **ecological education centre** (☎971 18 73 53; http://greenheartibiza.org; ⊙2-7pm Sun) enjoys an idyllic rural location, 9km southwest of Sant Rafel. It functions as both an experiential centre for permaculture techniques and the headquarters of the environmental charity Greenheart Ibiza. Tours can be arranged via its website's 'Contact Us' page.

Església de Sant Rafel

The Story Behind Ibiza's Clubs

The Ibiza Club Scene

In Ibiza, clubs historically 'leased' their premises to outside promoters on different nights. British dance brands introduced this initiative in the 1990s, at the height of the superclub era, when cash-rich clubs such as Ministry of Sound descended on the White Isle. Thursdays found Cream, from Liverpool, at Amnesia (p57) in Sant Rafel. We Love parties at the now-defunct Space (which held its final party in 2016) reached near-legendary status, with British promoters taking over the club for a 22-hour (8am to 6am!) marathon clubbing session. These leasing arrangements still continue to a degree, but today Ibiza's clubs prefer to promote their own nights, working directly with DJs.

Manumission Mania

The most successful outside promoter in Ibiza's clubbing history was undoubtedly Manumission (Latin for 'freedom from slavery'), resident at Sant Rafel's Privilege (p57) between 1994 and 2006. On Manumission nights, the venue regularly pulled in 10,000 clubbers. Manumission started as a gay night in Manchester, but after violent threats from gangsters it relocated to Ibiza. The team consisted of two brothers, Andy and Mike McKay, and their partners Dawn and Claire, plus an army of PR people. Instead of paying skyrocketing fees to superstar DJs, they created a fantasy event at Privilege, with acrobats, circus performers, cabaret, actors, dancers and even a DJ in the toilets. The night climaxed with a live sex show starring Mike and Claire. Unsurprisingly the British and Spanish press granted Manumission an avalanche of publicity: journalistic outrage sparked record ticket sales and resulted in a packed-out club (though the sex shows were only actually staged until 1999).

After a dispute with Privilege, Manumission briefly moved across the road to Amnesia, but tensions between the brothers led to a split. Andy and Dawn later set up the very successful Ibiza Rocks, introducing live bands to Ibiza and turning the famous hotel Pikes (p127) into a key party venue. Mike and Claire returned to the clubbing arena with a night called Phantasmagoria in the 2013 and 2014 seasons, but the event suffered licensing issues. Both couples still live in Ibiza.

Explore ⊚
South Ibiza

The island's spectacular southern reaches include Ibiza's highest peak (Sa Talaiassa; 475m), its most beautiful snow-white-sand beaches and the enigmatic, enticing southwest islet of Es Vedrà. It's a region of legends, both ancient and modern, with a contemporary clifftop art installation called Stonehenge and the mystical sight of Atlantis. Factor in the world-renowned clubs of Platja d'en Bossa, some top-notch restaurants and bombastic beach bars, and the glistening salt flats of the World Heritage–listed Parc Natural de Ses Salines, and the allure of Ibiza's south is unique.

The southeast's big highlight is Ses Salines, home to splendid white sands and mellow chiringuitos (beach bars) on Platja de Ses Salines and Es Cavallet, and the shimmering Salines salt pans (especially glorious at sunset).

Getting There & Around

🚌 L3 Ibiza Town–Sant Rafel–Sant Antoni (every 15 to 60 minutes).

🚌 L8 Ibiza Town–Sant Josep–Sant Antoni (hourly).

🚌 L10 Airport–Platja d'en Bossa–Ibiza Town (every 20 to 30 minutes).

🚌 From May to October, buses link Ibiza Town and Sant Antoni with southern beaches.

South Ibiza Map on p72

Cala d'Hort (p63) SBEDAUX/SHUTTERSTOCK ©

Top Experience 📷

Discover the Myths of Es Vedrà & its surrounds

The scenery around Ibiza's southwestern tip is breathtaking. The spectacular islet of Es Vedrà rises from the azure Mediterranean, guarded by its dragon-like sister islet, Es Vedranell. Almost opposite is the beautiful beach of Cala d'Hort, while just southeast lie the evocatively situated Torre des Savinar defence tower and the simply extraordinary old quarry known as Atlantis.

◎ MAP P72, A3

There's no bus service to the area, so you'll need your own wheels.

Rock Star

The exquisite, vertiginous island of **Es Vedrà** is one of the most startling sights in the Balearics, emerging abruptly from the glittering Mediterranean like an offshore volcano. It's associated with numerous local legends, from sirens to UFOs to the Virgin Mary. Since Ibiza's southern-coast road is surrounded by high mountains, the effect is spellbinding when Es Vedrà unexpectedly pops into view.

You can't visit the island itself, but you can access the main Es Vedrà viewpoint: a rocky dirt track leads off the signposted Torre des Savinar turn-off (1km southeast of Cala d'Hort), then it's a 10-minute stroll.

Torre des Savinar

The lofty, spectacularly located **Torre des Savinar** (Map p72, B3) defence tower boasts sweeping views directly over the enigmatic islets of Es Vedrà and Es Vedranell, and southeast to pancake-flat Formentera. It was constructed in 1763 to safeguard Ibiza's southern flank from pirate attacks – it's also known as Torre d'en Pirata. The tower is a 10-minute walk uphill from the main Es Vedrà viewpoint.

Cala d'Hort

Nestled beneath the steep wooded hills of Ibiza's isolated southwest corner, opposite Es Vedrà, bijou Cala d'Hort enjoys a privileged, tucked-away location. The beach is an arc of sand sprinkled with pebbles and rocks, with quieter areas to the north and south, and three good shoreside restaurants.

Cala d'Hort is part of the **Reserva Natural de Cala d'Hort**, which was established after a drawn-out campaign against developers' plans to build a golf course and 420-bed hotel complex in this beautiful region. The project prompted huge demonstrations: 12,000 people marched against it in 1999 and the bulldozers

★ Top Tips

o The main Es Vedrà viewpoint is only accessible on foot, as are the caves, the Torre des Savinar and Atlantis. Take the Torre des Savinar turn-off 1km southeast of Cala d'Hort; park after 500m (it's a bumpy track) and walk the final 10 minutes to the viewpoint, or continue up to the tower.

o Atlantis and the two caves are revered by the spiritually minded, and should be treated with respect.

✕ Take a Break

On Cala d'Hort, El Carmen (p77) specialises in fresh fish and rice dishes.

Es Boldadó (p74) serves up more of the same, with even better views.

The Many Myths of Es Vedrà

The subject of countless local myths and legends, the island of Es Vedrà is perhaps Ibiza's most enigmatic attraction. It's said to be highly magnetic (sailors have reported malfunctioning compasses as they near the island) and there have supposedly been numerous UFO sightings in the area. A pilot even diverted his flight to make an emergency landing in Valencia in 1979 after reporting strange lights and an unidentified object around Es Vedrà.

The island is also linked to the Carthaginian love and fertility goddess, Tanit. Another story has it that Es Vedrà could be the island of the sirens – the sea-nymphs who tried to lure Odysseus from his ship in Homer's epic. A Carmelite priest, Francesc Palau i Quer, reported seeing visions of the Virgin Mary and satanic rituals here in the 19th century.

were stopped in 2002, with the creation of the nature reserve.

Atlantis

A tiny rocky peninsula, remarkable **Atlantis** (Pedrera de Cala d'Hort; Map p72, B3) is actually a former quarry, but it's easy to see how hippies viewed the oblique cut-stone outlines as the remains of a lost civilisation. Visitors have added Hindu-style carvings to the rocks, and cliff jumpers plunge into the deep, cobalt water. It's only accessible on foot, a hard-going 30-minute descent southeast from the parking spot near the Es Vedrà viewpoint and Torre des Savinar.

Caves

There are two separate caves gazing out on Es Vedrà. The **Cova des Mirador** (Map p72, B3) is a tiny cavern directly below the main Es Vedrà viewpoint; many people leave offerings here. Just above Atlantis is the **Cova de Buda** (Map p72, B3), a place of sanctuary that's home to a remarkable Buddha image said to have been etched decades ago by a Japanese hermit.

Es Vedranell

Guarding its bigger sister Es Vedrà like a demon from a fantasy novel, the small **island** of Es Vedranell is a jumble of jagged rocks. Its nickname, 'sleeping dragon', is fully justified – it's easy to pick out its head and spiky backbone emerging from the water.

Top Experience 📷
See the Sparkling Ses Salines Salt Pans

The southeastern tip of Ibiza offers some seriously stunning landscapes, including two of the island's very best silky-sand beaches. Most of this region is protected by the Parc Natural de Ses Salines and taken up with a dazzling expanse of colour-shifting salt pans. To their east and south are the back-to-back, bleach-blonde beaches of Ses Salines and (gay-friendly) Es Cavallet.

◉ MAP P72, E4

Bus L11 and L11B link Ibiza Town with Platja de Ses Salines (€2.90, 25 minutes, half-hourly to hourly May to October, twice daily Monday, Wednesday and Friday November to April).

Parc Natural de Ses Salines

Encompassing southeastern Ibiza and stretching south across the water to northern Formentera, the 168-sq-km World Heritage–listed **Parc Natural de Ses Salines** (☎ 971 17 76 88; www.balearsnatura.com) comprises marshes, sparkling salt pans, sandy cream-coloured beaches and pine-cloaked coastal cliffs. It's a safe haven for 210 species of birds, such as the Audouin's gull, the Balearic shearwater and hot-pink flocks of migrating flamingos (August to October).

Platja de Ses Salines

Arguably Ibiza's best **beach**, Platja de Ses Salines is a gorgeous sweep of white sand with clear sea, backed by rolling sand dunes, patches of sabina pine woodland and buzzy *chiringuitos*. Sunseekers of all kinds flock here to work the bronzed, blissed-out Ibiza look. The scene varies from northwest (family friendly) to southeast (with a more boho vibe and some nudism).

Torre de Ses Portes

From this formidable 18th-century **defence tower** on Ibiza's southernmost tip (a 20-minute walk from the south end of Es Cavallet or Platja de Ses Salines), you'll glimpse the islands that speckle the Es Freus strait separating Ibiza and Formentera. Among them are Illa des Penjats (Hangman's Island), where captured pirates were once sent to the gallows, and Illa des Porcs (Pigs' Island), where plump pigs smuggled over from Formentera were once kept.

Ses Salines Salt Pans

Just south of Ibiza's airport, the shimmering pools of the **salines** (salt pans) were the island's main source of wealth until the tourism boom. Approaching Platja de Ses Salines and Es Cavallet, you drive right across the salt flats' main body, an unforgettable experience. Salt is still harvested here for export; you'll see it piled up by the road.

★ Top Tips

o There are large car parks (per day €6) at both Platja de Ses Salines and Es Cavallet. They fill up quickly between mid-June and September, so arrive early.

o On the 20-minute walk from Es Cavallet or Platja de Ses Salines to the Torre de Ses Portes, there's no shade and nowhere for refreshments; bring water.

o Meals and drinks are expensive at the beachside *chiringuitos;* consider packing a picnic.

✗ Take a Break

On Platja de Ses Salines, Sa Trinxa (p79) is one of Ibiza's best places to chill, with daily DJs.

On Es Cavallet, La Escollera (p77) is a stylish bar-restaurant with lovely views over the Mediterranean.

Walking Tour 🥾

Platja d'en Bossa to Platja de Ses Salines

This southern-Ibiza walk cuts through a diverse landscape that takes in wooded hills and three of the island's best white beaches, and fringes some glistening salt flats, mostly within the Unesco-listed Parc Natural de Ses Salines. There are a couple of landmark defence towers to admire along the way, and the sea views are outstanding.

Walk Facts

Start South end of Platja d'en Bossa

Finish Northwestern end of Platja de Ses Salines

Length 7km; three hours

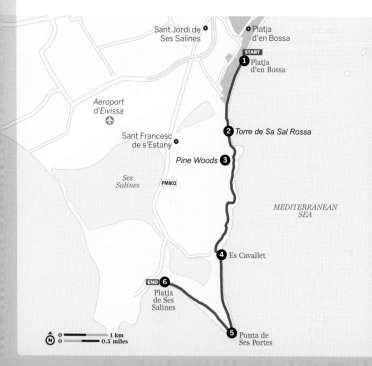

❶ Platja d'en Bossa

The southern end of **Platja d'en Bossa** (p78) is by far the most attractive stretch of this popular, touristed party beach, with sand dunes and, so far, relatively limited tourist development. You'll enjoy fine views back along the coast to Ibiza Town and **Dalt Vila**.

❷ Torre de Sa Sal Rossa

Just beyond the far southern tip of Platja d'en Bossa, this conical **defence tower** was constructed in the 16th century to safeguard Ibiza's salt trade. The bay just below, **Cala de Sa Sal Rossa** (Pink Salt Cove), was a tiny port until the 19th century. Rowing boats loaded with salt would shuttle back and forth to cargo ships anchored offshore.

❸ Pine Forests

This next section offers some shade, and leaves behind Ibiza's tourist scene. From the Torre de Sa Sal Rossa, a path climbs up the **pine-forested hills**. This well-defined, undulating track parallels the coast south for 3km, passing deserted rocky coves. The path doesn't stray more than 50m or so from the coast, so it's impossible to get lost.

❹ Es Cavallet

Eventually, you'll emerge at **Es Cavallet** (p73) beach, close to **La Escollera** (p77) restaurant. There's little shade ahead, so consider stopping for a drink and a bite here. Then it's a straight walk south along the blonde-sand shore. The southern end of Es Cavallet is very popular with gay visitors and nudists, and has a great gay-focused restaurant, **Chiringay** (p76).

❺ Punta de Ses Portes

South of Chiringay, the shoreline turns rocky as you approach the evocative **Punta de Ses Portes**, Ibiza's southernmost tip. There's a tiny cove here, and unparalleled views south across the sea to Formentera. Standing guard over this lookout is the 18th-century **Torre de Ses Portes** (p67).

❻ Platja de Ses Salines

From the tower, return up the western side of the peninsula towards **Platja de Ses Salines** (p66). You'll pass several tiny coves and rocky outcrops bordered by pines. This is Ibiza's premier patch of frost-white sand, dotted with several uber-fashionable bars and restaurants. There's a bus stop at the northwest end of the beach.

✖ Take a Break

Es Cavallet and Platja de Ses Salines both have beachside *chiringuitos*. On Salines, **Sa Trinxa** (p79) is one of Ibiza's best. Over on Es Cavallet, stylish **La Escollera** (p77) is brilliant for seafood, while barefoot-chic **El Chiringuito** (⌨971 39 53 55; www.elchiringuitoibiza.com; Es Cavallet; mains €25-39; ⏱10am-midnight mid-Apr–mid-Oct) and gay-friendly **Chiringay** (p76) offer popular Mediterranean menus.

Driving Tour

Road-Tripping Southern Coves & Villages

This south-coast spin takes in glorious hidden coves, a couple of pretty villages, an archaeological site, Ibiza's loftiest peak, outstanding modern sculpture and sensational coastal scenery, weaving through orchards, olive groves and wooded hills along the way. If you time your arrival at Stonehenge for sunset, so much the better.

Trip Facts

Start Sant Francesc de s'Estany

Finish Stonehenge

Length 45km

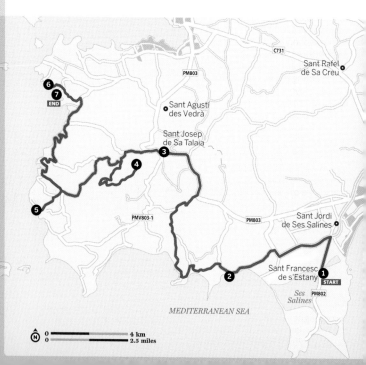

❶ Sant Francesc de s'Estany

The little village of **Sant Francesc de s'Estany**, 6km southwest of Ibiza Town, was a base for the workers of the surrounding *salines*. Learn about the history of the local salt trade and environment at the **Centre d'Interpretació de Ses Salines** (☑ 971 17 76 88; Sant Francesc de s'Estany; admission free; ⏲ 10am-2pm & 6-9pm Wed-Sun Jun-Sep, 10am-2pm Sat & Sun Oct-May).

❷ Sa Caleta

The cliffside **Poblament Fenici de Sa Caleta** (Platja de Sa Caleta; admission free) was the first human settlement on Ibiza. In the early 8th century BC, the Carthaginians established a foothold here, constructing a small hamlet by the sea. Beyond metal railings and basic information panels lie building foundations, though the site isn't all that visually impressive. It's a five-minute walk southeast of **Platja de Sa Caleta** (p73).

❸ Sant Josep de Sa Talaia

The village of **Sant Josep** centres on a pretty main street with an attractive, whitewashed 1726 **church** (Plaça de l'Església; ⏲ hours vary) boasting a three-storey facade with an impressive front porch. There are also some wonderfully low-key cafes, restaurants and boutiques.

❹ Sa Talaiassa

Ibiza's highest peak, **Sa Talaiassa** (Sa Talaia), lords it over the island's south at 475m. Drive to the summit (signposted from the Sant Josep–Cala Vedella road) or hike up on a signed 2.5km trail from Sant Josep. The summit has amazing vistas over the island, though you'll be peering between gaps in the pine forest.

❺ Cala Carbó

There's little to **Cala Carbó**, a pretty niche in Ibiza's southwest coast (9km southwest of Sant Josep), its shoreline a mix of sand and pebbles. You'll find good snorkelling offshore and a couple of popular seafood restaurants here.

❻ Cala Codolar

Cliff-flanked **Cala Codolar** is a tiny, sheltered sandy beach at the end of a fiddly (signposted) dirt track, southwest off the Platges de Comte road. The headland to the north prevents the water from getting too choppy, and there's a summer *chiringuito*.

❼ Stonehenge

Ibiza's most contemporary attraction is a stunning open-air clifftop monument that locals have named **Stonehenge** (Time and Space – The Speed of Light; Cala Codolar; admission free; ⏲ 24hr). A semicircle of 13 basalt columns, it was created by Australian artist Andrew Rogers and commissioned by Cirque du Soleil founder Guy Laliberté.

Stonehenge stands on a rocky coastal shelf, a 10-minute (unsigned) walk south of Cala Codolar.

South Ibiza

For reviews see
- ◆ Top Experiences   p62
- ⊙ Experiences   p73
- ✕ Eating   p74
- 🍷 Drinking   p78
- 🛍 Shopping   p79

CT33

CT31

1

2

3

4

Sant Rafel
de Sa Creu ●

Sant Agustí
des Vedrà ●

Sant Josep
de Sa Talaia

Racó
Verd

10 ⊙ ✕ **16**

▲ Sa Talaiassa
(475m)

PM803

PM803

Es Cubells
Esglèsia de ⊙ Es Cubells
Torre des **4** ⊙
Cova des Savinar
Mirador Cova de Buda
Atlantis ● ● ●
2 ⊙ Cala
Llentrisca

Cap
Llentrisca

Es Vedranell

Es Vedrà ◆

Cala
Vedella

Cala ⊙ **5**
Carbó
✕ **8**
Cala d'Hort 🍷 **14**

Platges
de Comte ⊙

Cala
Codolar

Cala **6** ⊙
Tarida

Ibiza Town

Figueretes ●

Platja
d'en Bossa

Platja
d'en Bossa

Sant Jordi de
Ses Salines

23 🛍 **7** ⊙
Esglèsia de ⊙
Sant Jordi

Aeroport
d'Eivissa ✈

Sant Francesc
de s'Estany ●

18
9 ✕ 🛍 **11**
17 ✕
19 ✕

Ses
Salines ⊙

Pare Natural
de Ses Salines 🌳
21 🍷

PM802

15 ✕
⊙ Es Cavallet
1 ◆
20 ⊙ ✕ **12**
🛍 Torre de
Punta de 🍷 Ses Portes
Ses Portes

Platja de
Ses Salines ⊙

22 🛍

Platja
de ⊙ **3**
Sa Caleta

13 ✕

M E D I T E R R A N E A N   S E A

A **B** **C** **D** **E** **F**

🔄 N
0 ⊢——⊣ 5 km
0 ⊢——⊣ 2.5 miles

Experiences

Es Cavallet BEACH

1  MAP P72, E4

On the eastern side of a slender peninsula, the wonderful, wild-feel, salt-white beach of Es Cavallet is one of the island's most perfect strips of sand. It was designated Ibiza's first naturist beach in 1978; today it's the island's main gay beach. The northern section is more family-geared, while the southern half is almost exclusively gay.

Cala Llentrisca BEACH

2  MAP P72, B3

This sublime little horseshoe bay, backed by wooded hills, isn't accessible by road, but it's only a 10-minute walk from the nearest parking spot, 4km southwest of Es Cubells village – you'll hit a private *urbanización* (residential area) barrier, but you should be allowed through to reach this exquisite beach. There are a few fishermen's huts by the shore, but it's mostly blissfully peaceful, with just the brilliant-blue sea lapping the pebble shoreline to break the sound of silence.

Platja de Sa Caleta BEACH

3  MAP P72, D3

Sa Caleta, 3.5km west of the airport (though you wouldn't know it), consists of three little beaches: the main one has golden sand, with loungers and umbrellas to rent, while the two others are tiny, pebbly and more secluded.

Església Es Cubells (p74)

Església Es Cubells CHURCH

4 ◎ MAP P72, C3

This gleaming-white, classically Ibizan 19th-century church is poised majestically atop towering seaside cliffs in the tiny south-coast village of Es Cubells, enjoying jaw-droppingly beautiful views across the Mediterranean. (Es Cubells; ⊗hours vary)

Cala Vedella BEACH

5 ◎ MAP P72, B2

One of Ibiza's most sheltered, attractive bays, cliff-framed Cala Vedella lies at the rear of a deep inlet. It's an upmarket resort perfect for families, with a powdery white-sand beach, shallow water, several restaurants, a dive school, SUP outlets and sunbeds. Dotted around are low-rise hotels, hillside villas and yachts gracing the turquoise sea.

Bus L26 runs to/from Ibiza Town (€2.90, 45 minutes) four times daily mid-May to mid-October via Sant Josep.

Cala Tarida BEACH

6 ◎ MAP P72, B1

The beautiful bay of Cala Tarida boasts two gold-sand beaches and is surrounded by villas, family-friendly low-rise hotels and the swanky Cotton Beach Club. It's a lovely scene, though very busy in summer and quite developed.

Bus L38 runs to/from Ibiza Town (€2.90, 45 minutes, three daily June to mid-October), and bus L5 runs to/from Sant Antoni

(€2.90, 35 minutes, eight daily May to October).

Església de Sant Jordi CHURCH

7 ◎ MAP P72, E3

Incongruously located in the suburbs 4km southwest of Ibiza Town, the fortress-like Església de Sant Jordi is well worth a quick diversion. A chapel has stood here since the 13th century, though the impressive present structure – its colossal white walls topped with full battlements to deter pirates – dates from the late 16th century. (Plaça de l'Església, Sant Jordi de Ses Salines; ⊗dawn-dusk, hours vary)

Eating

Es Boldadó SEAFOOD, IBIZAN €€

8 ✕ MAP P72, B3

Book a terrace table for sunset and you'll enjoy one of Ibiza's most dramatic dining locations, with views over mystical Es Vedrà island. Es Boldadó is renowned for its seafood; you can't beat the clams or steamed mussels, followed by grilled grouper fish. Or go for paella, *bullit de peix* (fish stew) or *arròs a la marinera* (fishermen's rice). (☑626 494537; www.restauranteesboldadoibiza.es; Cala d'Hort; mains €15-35; ⊗1-4pm & 7.30-11pm, reduced hours Nov-Apr)

Restaurante Sa Caleta SEAFOOD €€

A fine all-year seafood restaurant (see 3 ✕ Map p72, D3), tucked into the back of a popular beach (p73) since 1988. Fish is grilled or

Ibiza's Salt Pans

Original Salt-Makers

First developed by the Phoenicians, Ibiza's spectacular, glittering salt pans were the island's only reliable source of income for over 2000 years. The Romans and other invaders maintained the pools, but it was the Moors, experts in hydraulic technology, who developed the sophisticated system of channels, mills and sluice gates. Originally, salt was traded from nearby Platja d'en Bossa, from a bay called Sal Rossa (Pink Salt), but in the late 19th century a new jetty was built at La Canal on the north side of Platja de Ses Salines and a steam engine was brought in to shift the salt. Until that time, everything had been done manually, with labourers toiling in the extreme August heat. These days, tractors, trucks and conveyor belts do the hard work.

Salt has been of vital importance since antiquity, essential for health and preserving food, and southern Ibiza's terrain is ideal for salt production. Sea water is pumped in during May, left to evaporate for three months and then harvested in August. The water level must be perfect: if it evaporates too quickly there will be no salt residue. Rainy summers also harm salt production because if the water isn't saline enough it won't crystallise into salt. If conditions are good, a crust of pink-white powder develops; this is stored in huge salt mounds, then exported.

Ibiza's natural salt is a popular souvenir. You'll spot its pretty turquoise packaging at shops all over the island, including the **Sal de Ibiza boutique** (p79) on the Eivissa–Sant Josep road.

Natural Reserve

Ibiza's salt flats, which cover 400 hectares, form part of the World Heritage–listed **Parc Natural de Ses Salines** (p67), a 168-sq-km nature reserve that takes in southeastern Ibiza and northern Formentera. The salt pans are an important wetland habitat for birds and a refuelling stop for migrating storks, herons and flamingos. Over 200 bird species have been documented here, with year-round residents including ospreys and black-necked grebes. Sant Francesc de s'Estany's **Centre d'Interpretació de Ses Salines** (p71) delves into the Ses Salines environment and salt trade.

baked, and there's good paella. Summer sees the arrival of a low-key garden bar-restaurant (same menu), plus regular live music.

Don't miss trying *café Caleta* (p76)– this house speciality is infused with herbs, lemon and orange peel and a good splash

of brandy. (☑971 18 70 95; www.
restaurantesacaleta.com; Platja de Sa
Caleta; mains €14-34; ⏲1pm-midnight
May-Oct, 1-7pm Nov-Apr)

Passion

HEALTH FOOD €€

9 MAP P72, E3

For the ultimate morning-after
pick-me-up, this outpost of Ibiza's
favourite healthy-eating cafe chain
serves fabulous fresh breakfasts
(omelettes, granola pots, three
varieties of smashed avocado) and
fitness-focused mains (pastas, salads, wraps), almost all organic and
vegetarian or vegan, and always
packed with flavour. Or just grab
a juice or smoothie to go. There's
often a queue out the door. (☑971
30 51 30; www.passion-ibiza.com;
Avinguda Platja d'en Bossa; breakfasts
€6.50-15, mains €9-16; ⏲9am-11pm
late Apr–mid-Oct; 🛜🖊)

Destino

TAPAS €

10 MAP P72, C2

Offering arguably some of the
island's best tapas, this excellent
though small place has lots of
unusual, interesting dishes, very
moderate prices, some Moroccan
flavours and plenty of choice for
vegetarians. Eat on the little terrace
overlooking pretty Sant Josep or in
the atmospheric dining room. It's
always very busy; book ahead on
summer nights. (☑971 80 03 41; Carrer Sa Talaia 15, Sant Josep de Sa Talaia;
tapas €4-10; ⏲1pm-1am Mon-Sat; 🖊)

Beachouse

INTERNATIONAL €€€

11 MAP P72, E3

Is it a bar? Beach club? Boutique?
Restaurant? Beachouse is all
of these, in one stylish unit on a
prime patch of shoreside real estate at the southern end of Platja
d'en Bossa. The food is excellent
(salads, pizzas, pastas, succulent
meats), the crowd is fashionable,
the DJs are world-class, and the
drinks and sunbeds are suitably
high-end. (☑971 39 68 58; www.
beachouseibiza.com; mains €14-24;
⏲10am-midnight Apr–mid-Oct; 🛜)

Chiringay

MEDITERRANEAN €€€

12 MAP P72, E4

Perched on white sands towards
the southern end of Es Cavallet,
Chiringay is a lively gay-scene *chiringuito* with stylish white-and-tur-

---

Café Caleta

In restaurants across Ibiza,
particularly in the south, you
might come across *café
Caleta,* a special *queimada*
(Spanish alcoholic punch).
Making a memorable end to a
meal (unless you're the driver),
it's wonderfully aromatic and
includes spices, lemon and
orange peel and a generous
dose of brandy. The *café Caleta*
is said to have been invented
back in the 1950s by the owner
of Restaurante Sa Caleta (p74)
on the south coast, and is
probably best sampled in its
original location.

quoise decor and DJ sessions from 4pm. It does an impressive line of Spanish-Mediterranean dishes, including paellas, giant salads and a delicious tuna with avocado dressing. It's a 15-minute walk from the Es Cavallet or Platja de Ses Salines car parks. (☎971 59 95 08; http://chiringay.com; Es Cavallet; mains €18-26; ☺10am-8pm May–mid-Oct)

Es Torrent SEAFOOD €€€

13 MAP P72, C3

Popular with a yachtie crowd, this excellent seafood restaurant is pocketed away on a pretty, hidden rocky cove, 8km south of Sant Josep. Along with the full menu, staff will inform you about which fresh fish and other seafood dishes are available. Specialities include *fideuà* (paella-like fish-and-seafood noodle dish) and *bullit de peix*. (☎971 80 21 60; www.estorrent.net; Es Torrent; mains €25-40; ☺1-10pm Easter–mid-Oct)

El Carmen SEAFOOD €€€

14 MAP P72, B3

With tables directly overlooking Es Vedrà and sandy-pebbly Cala d'Hort, El Carmen is highly popular for good reason. It offers lots of seafood and fresh fish (grilled or baked, often as sharing plates for two), delectable rice dishes and *fideuà,* and tasty local bread and aioli, plus omelettes, salads and a small kids' menu. (☎971 18 74 49; http://elcarmencaladhort.com; Cala d'Hort; mains €17-36; ☺1-10pm mid-Mar–late Oct; 🚼)

Es Torrent

One of Ibiza's secret coves, Es Torrent is 8km south of Sant Josep on the west side of the Porroig promontory. Its name comes from its position at the end of a torrent (seasonal riverbed). Beyond the sandy shoreline, the sea is shallow and a striking shade of blue. There's good snorkelling around the cliffs fringing the bay.

La Escollera SPANISH, INTERNATIONAL €€€

15 MAP P72, E4

On the northern tip of Es Cavallet, this beach-chic, seafood-focused, year-round bar-restaurant has delicious views over white sands and across to Formentera from its terrace. Signature dishes include wild sea bass and an impressive range of paellas for sharing (with veggie options), though there are also meats such as steaks and country-style chicken. You'll probably want to make a reservation in summer. (☎971 39 65 72; www.laescolleraibiza.com; Es Cavallet; mains €15-35; ☺1-11pm Jul & Aug, 1-6pm Sep-Jun; 🛜🚲)

Can Berri Vell SPANISH €€

16 MAP P72, C1

Set inside a 17th-century Ibizan *casament* (farmhouse), this highly atmospheric restaurant sprawls across a warren of rooms, with lots of historic features to admire,

Platja d'en Bossa

For decades, pale-gold **Platja d'en Bossa** (Map p72, E3), 5km southwest of Ibiza Town, was a pretty conventional bucket-and-spade resort aimed at holidaying families, but recent developments by the land-owning Matutes family have revolutionised the place. It's now a non-stop party spot hosting some seriously big-name DJs, mostly thanks to the opening of the glitzy daytime club/hotel **Ushuaïa** and the launch of **Hï Ibiza** on the site of legendary, now-defunct superclub Space.

including metre-thick walls. There's also a lovely terrace with views over Sant Agustí's village church. The cuisine is quite elaborate, with seasonal specials and dishes such as roasted turbot with caramelised carrots and white truffles. (☎971 34 43 21; www.canberrivell.es; Plaça Major, Sant Agustí des Vedrà; mains €15-27; ⏰8pm-midnight Apr-Oct, closed Sun Apr & May)

Drinking

Hï Ibiza   CLUB

18 🚇 MAP P72, E3

A glitzy addition to Ibiza's super-club scene, Hï is part of the ever-growing Ushuaïa empire. Refreshing the site originally occupied by Ibizan clubbing institution Space,

it has cocktail menus, two main rooms, neon-tastic nightly changing light shows, a bathroom DJ and a chic, tepee-dotted open-air garden. DJs Martin Garrix, Eric Prydz and Armin van Buuren have had residencies here. (www.hiibiza.com; Carretera de Platja d'en Bossa; €45-60; ⏰midnight-6am Jun-early Oct)

Ushuaïa   CLUB

18 🚇 MAP P72, E3

Queen of daytime clubbing, ice-cool Ushuaïa is an open-air mega-club, packed with designer-clad hedonistas and waterside fun. The party starts early, with superstar DJs such as David Guetta, Martin Garrix, Luciano and Robin Schulz, and poolside lounging on Bali-style beds. Check out the Sky Lounge for sparkling sea views, or stay the night in the minimalist-chic hotel. (☎971 92 81 93; www.ushuaiabeach hotel.com; Platja d'en Bossa 10; €40-100; ⏰3pm or 5pm-midnight May-Oct; 📶)

DC 10   CLUB

19 🚇 MAP P72, E3

The rawest, least pretentious club in Ibiza, right by the airport runway, DC 10 is all about the music and has a distinctly underground vibe. The door tax is relatively modest (for Ibiza!) and drinks are moderately priced compared to other big venues. Come for Circo Loco (Mondays), one of the island's best sessions, kicking off early in the day. (Carretera Sant Jordi-Ses Salines Km 1; admission €20-40; ⏰3pm-6am May–mid-Oct)

Sa Trinxa

BAR

20 MAP P72, E4

At the southeastern end of Platja de Ses Salines, a hefty (worthwhile) walk from the parking, this is the island's coolest *chiringuito*. It draws quite a crowd – hardcore clubbers and fashionistas, Ibizan hippy types and the odd model – all soaking up the Balearic vibes of resident DJs that include Jon Sa Trinxa. Contemporary Spanish-international snacks and meals are served, too. (www.satrinxa.com; Platja de Ses Salines; ⊙11am-9pm May-Oct)

Experimental Beach

BAR

21 MAP P72, E4

Hidden away on a secluded, spectacularly positioned headland overlooking Ses Salines natural park, fashionable Experimental Beach is a mellow cocktail bar, beachy lounge space, modern Spanish-international restaurant (mains €25 to €35) and upmarket boutique all rolled into one. The sea-and-salt-pan panoramas are something special. It's signposted just south of Sant Francesc de s'Estany. (☑664 331269; www.eccbeach.com; Ses Salines; ⊙1pm-late May–mid-Oct)

Shopping

Sal de Ibiza

FOOD, CLOTHING

22 MAP P72, D3

Amid turquoise-tastic design, savour salty treats made with all-natural sea salt harvested from Ibiza's glittering Ses Salines natural park. Salts are flavoured with hibiscus, ginger or chilli, while Ibizan wines and honeys fill the shelves. There are also scented candles, Campos de Ibiza toiletries, and floaty dresses and shirts. It's 5.5km southeast of Sant Josep, en route to Ibiza Town. (www.saldeibiza.com; Carretera Eivissa-Sant Josep Km 6.5; ⊙10am-9pm mid-Apr–Oct)

Vino & Co

WINE

23 MAP P72, E3

A wine specialist, often with more than 30 wines open for tasting, including many Ibizan bottles. It also has a bar for lingering over tapas. Check the Facebook page for upcoming events. It's 4.5km southwest of Ibiza Town. (☑971 30 53 24; www.facebook.com/VinoyColbiza; Carretera Eivissa-Sant Josep Km 1.6; ⊙4-10pm Mon-Thu, to midnight Fri; 🛜)

South Ibiza Shopping

Racó Verd

Almost opposite the village church, this gorgeous garden **cafe-bar-restaurant** (Map p72, C2; ☑971 80 02 67; www.racoverdibiza.es; Plaça de l'Església, Sant Josep de sa Talaia; dishes €5.50-17; ⊙10am-2am Mar-Nov; 🛜) is the hub of the community, hosting regular live-music events (flamenco, jazz, rock, DJ sets). It's fab for à la carte breakfasts (try the spicy Mexican-style eggs), ciabatta sandwiches and a few tapas (some Mexican-inspired), or just a beer, coffee or fresh juice at any time of day.

Explore

Santa Eulària des Riu & East Ibiza

A world away from the diehard party scene to its west and south, Santa Eulària des Riu (Ibiza's third-largest town) is a bustling yet attractive coastal resort with an easy-going vibe, a large marina, a fine seaside promenade, some good down-to-earth eateries and a small but beautiful historic quarter centred on its Puig de Missa hilltop. A string of lovely, lively beaches dot the coastline to the south and northeast, such as particularly charming Cala Mastella.

A collection of beachy jewels lie sprinkled along Ibiza's northeast coast, so allow time to find your perfect sweep of sand. Central Santa Eulària is ideal for casual drinks and a bite, or venture further afield, perhaps southwest to secluded Cala Sol d'en Serra for a magical modern-Mediterranean dinner.

Getting There & Around

🚌 L13 to/from Ibiza Town (€2, 25 minutes, every 20 to 60 minutes).

🚌 L19 to/from Sant Antoni (€2.35, 25 minutes, eight daily May to October, fewer November to April).

🚌 L24 to/from airport (€4, 45 minutes, hourly mid-May to mid-October).

⚓ Santa Eulalia Ferry runs summer-only ferries to/from Ibiza Town.

Santa Eulària des Riu & East Ibiza Map on p86

Top Experience 📷
Climb to the 16th-Century Fortress-Church

The hillock looming at the southwest end of Santa Eulària was a perfect retreat during the centuries when Ibiza was plagued by pirate attacks. Crowning its 52m summit is a remarkable 16th-century fortress-church with a defence tower. There are a couple of interesting museums here, too. The most scenic route up is via the stairs from Carrer de Sant Jaume.

Puig de Missa

⊙ MAP P86, B5

Puig de Missa is a 10-minute (600m) walk west of Santa Eulària's central Plaça d'Espanya.

Església de Puig de Missa

Sparkling high above town, this beautiful, whitewashed fortified **church** (⏰10am-6pm, Mass 11am Sun) dates from 1568. Its most impressive features are its defence tower (used as a shelter during pirate attacks) and 17th-century multi-arched entrance porch, complete with mighty supporting pillars. The interior is painted entirely white, except for the dramatic, golden, Churrigueresque-style (ornate style of baroque architecture) altar, dating to 1678.

Some historians believe Italian military engineer Giovanni Battista Calvi designed the church – he was also responsible for the majestic walls of Dalt Vila (p69) in Ibiza Town.

Museu Etnogràfic

Housed in a stunning old Puig de Missa *casa pagesa* (farmhouse), Santa Eulària's **ethnography museum** (Can Ros; 📞971 33 28 45; Avinguda del Pare Guasch; adult/child €3/free; ⏰10am-2pm & 5.30-8pm Mon-Sat, 11am-1.30pm Sun Apr-Sep, 10am-2pm Tue-Sat, 11am-1.30pm Sun Oct-Mar) concentrates on Ibiza's rural heritage. In its *porxo* (long room) are carpentry tools and musical instruments. Other exhibits include billowing wedding dresses, ceremonial necklaces, kitchen equipment, a wine cellar and a huge olive-oil press.

Can Planetes

Santa Eulària gets its suffix, 'des Riu' (of the river), from the reed-fringed stream just west of town. There's usually little more than a trickle of water, but it *is* the only river in the Balearics. The **interpretation centre** (Centre d'Interpretació del Riu de Santa Eulària; Passeig des Riu; admission free; ⏰10am-1pm Tue-Sat) in Can Planetes, a restored medieval Molí de Dalt mill, explains the irrigation systems first developed by the Moors and which flourished along Santa Eulària's riverbank. It's just off the Passeig des Riu (Riverbank Promenade), 600m northwest of Puig de Missa.

★ Top Tips

○ Bring water: there are no cafes, restaurants or shops on Puig de Missa.

○ It's best to visit in the morning, when the museums are guaranteed to be open and you can avoid the heat of the day.

○ The steps up to Puig de Missa are steep – those with mobility issues may struggle.

✕ Take a Break

In the heart of town, 10 minutes' walk from Puig de Missa, Can Cosmi (p92) is a great, locally loved spot for sensibly priced drinks and snacks.

A similar walk away, and gazing out on the seaside promenade, Passion (p89) has a fabulous line-up of health-focused juices, smoothies, breakfasts and other bites.

Walking Tour 🥾

Santa Eulària to Punta Arabí

The sparkling east-Ibiza coastline around Santa Eulària is rewarding to explore. Its indented shoreline is rich in coves, powdery beaches and low-key cafe-restaurants. This walk starts in urban surrounds at the southwestern end of Santa Eulària itself, then passes quiet sandy strands and patches of woodland. On the whole, it's easy to follow; you'll be right on the shore for most of the route, only having to skirt around the odd building.

Walk Facts

Start Santa Eulària promenade

Finish Punta Arabí

Length 5km; two hours

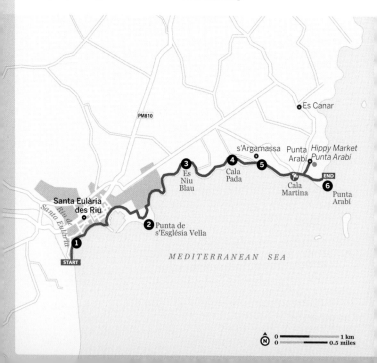

❶ Promenade

Begin your walk at the southwestern end of Santa Eulària, where the **Riu de Santa Eulària** meets the sea. Head east following Santa's lovely seafront promenade, and the two golden arcs of sand that make up the town's beach. You'll pass the excellent cafe **Passion** (p89), if you fancy an energy-boosting coffee or juice, or a tasty, soul-nourishing meal.

❷ Punta de s'Església Vella

A 10- to 15-minute walk northeast of Passion, you'll reach Santa's attractive marina (where there's a cluster of cafes and restaurants), then you'll approach the rocky promontory of **Punta de s'Església Vella**, which juts out into the Mediterranean. Legend has it that a medieval chapel once stood here, and that the structure collapsed seconds after the congregation departed Mass.

❸ Es Niu Blau

The walk loops around the land side of the Sol Beach House Ibiza hotel, and after 1.5km reaches the pretty beach of **Es Niu Blau** (also known as Platja de s'Estanyol). Here you'll find a 100m stretch of fine sand and the Pura Vida beach club, a swanky place that serves pricey fusion food.

❹ Cala Pada

The next section is partly shaded by coastal pines, and passes a couple of small promontories and some villas before reaching **Cala Pada** (p88). This laid-back beach has silky white sand, sun loungers, several cafe-restaurants, and boat links to Santa Eulària and Es Canar, making it an appealing stop-off point.

❺ S'Argamassa

The coastal path heads east through the pint-sized upmarket enclave of **S'Argamassa**, home to some large resort hotels. Just east of Nikki Beach Ibiza and the ME Ibiza hotel, seek out the surviving section of the **Roman S'Argamassa aqueduct**, dating from the 1st century AD and whose channelled water once fed a fish farm. Immediately east of S'Argamassa is the sandy bay of **Cala Martina**.

❻ Punta Arabí

From Cala Martina, you could explore the thickly wooded promontory of **Punta Arabí**, which sits opposite two tiny rocky islets. Or, if you head north towards Es Canar (about 1km away), you'll pass the site of the **Hippy Market Punta Arabí** (p93), Ibiza's original hippy market and now a sprawling, touristy and lively event held each Wednesday April to October.

🍴 Take a Break

The attractive bay of **Cala Pada** is a great place to refuel, with a good choice of restaurants right on the beach, or there's a boho beach shack, **Chirincana** (p91), on Cala Martina, around a kilometre east of here.

A **B** **C** **D**

↑ Sant Joan de
Labritja (5km)

N 0————— 2 km
0————— 1 mile

1

For reviews see	
👁 Top Experiences	p82
◉ Experiences	p87
✕ Eating	p89
🍺 Drinking	p92
🔒 Shopping	p92

PM810

Pou des
Lleó 🅐

Sant Carles
de Peralta ●

Cala Boix ✕ 13
🅐 3

Cala
Mastella ✕ 11
◉ 1

2

Cala
Llenya ◉ 2

PM810

Cala Nova ◉ 5

Es Canar ●

Riu de Santa Eulària

Cala
Pada
◉ 4

Punta
Arabí
◉

✕ 21
🔒

**Santa
Eulària
des Riu** ✕ 14
◉

Punta
Arabí

PM810

Punta de
s'Església Vella

✕ 17

See Santa Eulària
des Riu Enlargement

MEDITERRANEAN
SEA

4

PMV810-1 ● Valverde

Cala
Llonga 🅐 7
◉

Ibiza Town
(12km) 🅐 Cala Sol
9 d'en Serra

Santa Eulària des Riu

C Isidor
Macabich

Museu Etnogràfic

Església
de Puig
de Missa

C Sant Josep
Camí de Missa

15 C Sant Vicent

C Sant Jaume

C Sant
Llorenç

12 C Rodríguez 22 ◉
6 de Valcárcel C Sant
Joan

Plaça
d'Espanya 19 ✕

Pºg Marítim

Can Planetes

5

**Puig de
Missa**
◉

8 C del Mar

18

C Mariano
Riquer Wallis

Passeig de
s'Alamera

✕ 16

C Pintors
Puget

20

Playa de
Santa Eulalia

C Joan Tur Tur

Pºg Marítim

C Isidor
Macabich

6

10 ✕

Mediterranean
Sea

A **B** **C** **D**

Experiences

Cala Mastella BEACH

1 👁 MAP P86, D2

This little sandy cove is tucked into a deep inlet where pine trees reach down and almost kiss the emerald-green water, 9km northeast of Santa Eulària. Outside high season, you might have it to yourself. A seasonal kiosk serves mojitos and *bocadillos* (filled rolls). Scramble around the rocks at the beach's northeastern end to reach renowned seafood restaurant El Bigotes (p90).

Cala Llenya BEACH

2 👁 MAP P86, C2

About 9km northeast of Santa Eulària and 3km southeast of Sant Carles de Peralta, Cala Llenya is a serene, pine-fringed 200m-wide swathe of sand. It's popular with families, though never *too* crowded. Easterly breezes mean the waves can be strong from time to time. Bus 16A runs here from Sant Carles and Santa Eulària four times daily Monday to Saturday mid-May to mid-October.

Cala Boix BEACH

3 👁 MAP P86, D2

Below a highly scenic coastal road, 11km northeast of Santa Eulària, this slimline beach has coarse grey sand and pebbles. It's quite exposed, so things can get choppy if there's an easterly or northerly wind blowing. Steps lead down from the cliffs to the shore, where you'll find a few good restaurants and a straightforward *hostal*.

Cala Llenya

Cala Pada BEACH

4 ⊙ MAP P86, C3

About 3km northeast of Santa Eulària, bordered by pine groves and villas, this attractive beach has fine blonde sand and shallow water that's ideal for safe swimming. You'll find several café-restaurants and water-sports centres plus a dive school bordering the beach.

From May to October, Santa Eulalia Ferry (p150) runs three daily services linking Cala Pada with Santa Eulària (one way/return €12/6) and Ibiza Town (€20/11), plus one to two daily ferries to/from Formentera (return adult/child €34/18).

Cala Nova BEACH

5 ⊙ MAP P86, C2

Just 1km north of the resort of Es Canar (or 5km northeast of Santa Eulària), sandy, exposed, 250m-long Cala Nova sits pretty on a wide bay. The luxurious rural hotel **Atzaró** (☑971 33 88 38; www.atzaro. com; Carretera Santa Eulària-Sant Joan Km 15; r €495-545, ste €630-1190; P❄🤙🏊) has a year-round beach club here, and you can hire umbrellas and loungers right on the shore. During winter storms there's even some surf action.

Plaça d'Espanya SQUARE

6 ⊙ MAP P86, C5

Santa Eulària's central palm-studded square contains the town's

Santa Eulària's Backstory

There's some evidence of Roman settlement in the Santa Eulària region and, during the Moorish period, its river valley was cleverly irrigated and intensively farmed; find out more at **Can Planetes** (p83). The **Puig de Missa church** (p83) was built in the late 16th century, with houses cropping up around it during the 18th century.

But the town was still little more than an overgrown village until the 1930s, when American writer Elliot Paul spent an extended period here. He documented the outbreak of the Spanish Civil War on the island in his 1937 book *Life and Death of a Spanish Town* (a wonderful read). During the 1960s and '70s, Santa Eulària became something of a hang-out for a British thespian set, centred on the then-popular, now-defunct bar Sandy's. Terry-Thomas and Denholm Elliott bought homes in the area, and Laurence Olivier, Elizabeth Taylor and John Mills holidayed in the town.

Today's Santa Eulària is a curious mix of summer resort (complete with British pubs) and a regular Spanish town with a touch of historical charm.

dignified *ajuntament* (town hall), built in 1795; its arched frontal colonnade is flanked by two municipal coats of arms. Just off the square's northeast side is Santa Eulària's famous street of restaurants, Carrer Sant Vicent.

Cala Llonga   BEACH

 7 MAP P86, A4

Framed by high wooded headlands to the north and south, Cala Llonga is an attractive, sheltered east-coast bay with a lovely sandy beach. It's a primarily family-focused resort with wonderful swimming, but the town itself is blighted by high-rise hotels. It's 5km southwest of Santa Eulària.

Passeig de s'Alamera   STREET

 8 MAP P86, C5

Immediately southeast of Plaça d'Espanya, Santa Eulària's graceful main boulevard is lined with trees and cafes. On summer evenings, dozens of market stalls add a splash of colour, selling jewellery, artwork, clothing and local produce.

Eating

Amante   MEDITERRANEAN €€€

 9 MAP P86, A5

Gazing out over the Mediterranean from cliffs above a hidden cove, 1km southwest of Cala Llonga, Amante is one of Ibiza's most fashionable and romantic restaurants. During daylight it's a glitzy beach

Ibiza Town to Santa Eulària

The busy C733 and PM810 speed you northeast from Ibiza Town to Santa Eulària des Riu on the east coast. More scenic is the slower coastal PMV810-1 road via Cala Llonga, which winds through low hills and olive groves, with detours along the way to several beaches. To follow it, take the turn-off to Jesús 2km north of central Ibiza Town.

club (with €30 sun loungers), but from sunset it becomes an exquisitely beautiful place to dine, with a creative, delicious (if expensive) Spanish-Italian menu infused with home-grown ingredients.

The bar opens until 2am, and Amante hosts great movie nights every Tuesday evening in summer and events with DJs and dancing under the stars. Morning yoga classes are also on the menu. (📞971 19 61 76; www.amanteibiza. com; Cala Sol d'en Serra; mains €16-30; ⏰restaurant 11am-midnight mid-Apr–mid-Oct; 🛜)

Passion   HEALTH FOOD €€

 10 MAP P86, C6

With its sea-facing terrace, boho-cool styling and healthy-eating menu, this popular, fashionable cafe-restaurant specialises in predominantly vegetarian and raw food, such as black-bean burritos, butternut-squash salads and

beetroot burgers. It's perfect for breakfast (granola-yoghurt pots, avocado toast), a light lunch and even dinner. Or just grab a juice, smoothie, shake, protein punch or a slab of delicious homemade cake.

There are Passion branches sprinkled around the island, including at Ibiza Marina (p48) and Platja d'en Bossa (p76). (📞971 80 73 23; http://passion-ibiza.com; Carrer Joan Tur Tur 13; breakfasts €6.50-15, mains €9-16; ⏱9am-11pm May-Oct, to 5pm Nov-Apr; 🛜🍴)

El Bigotes   SEAFOOD €€

11 🍽 MAP P86, D2

Known far and wide, this simple, welcoming seafood shack juts out into glittering clear waters at the northeastern end of Cala Mastella. There are two daily sittings: noon

for grilled fish and 2pm for *bullit de peix* (fish stew with herbs, vegetables and potatoes). Finish with an Ibizan-special Caleta coffee. Book ahead by phone or in person. Cash only.

To get here, clamber over the rocks from Cala Mastella or, if driving along the coast to/from Cala Boix, take the signposted turn-off just east of the Cala Mastella turn-off. (📞650 797633; Cala Mastella; meals €25; ⏱noon-4pm Easter-Oct)

Es Terral   FRENCH, MEDITERRANEAN €€

12 🍽 MAP P86, C5

A cut above the competition on Santa's 'street of restaurants', Es Terral delivers sublime seafood and fish fuelled by French, Ibizan and organic ingredients, alongside informed, attentive service, courtesy of a husband-and-wife team. Try the fish of the day or one of the standout meat dishes, including Périgord duck breast, and roast chicken with *cava*-infused cabbage. (📞628 581314; Carrer Sant Vicent 47; mains €16-25; ⏱7-11.30pm Thu-Tue Apr-Oct, 12.30-3.30pm & 7-11pm Thu-Sun Nov, Dec & Mar, closed Jan & Feb)

La Noria   SEAFOOD €€

13 🍽 MAP P86, D2

Offering a dreamy outlook from the Mediterranean from its terrace perched above Cala Boix, this popular restaurant is known for its seafood, with excellent paella (€44 to €60 for two, order ahead), grilled fish and *bullit de*

KITTICHET TUNGSUBPHOKIN/SHUTTERSTOCK ©

peix. It also has a good selection of Ibizan wines. At its best for sunset dinners. (📞971 33 53 97; Cala Boix; mains €14-30; ⏱1-4pm & 7.30-10.30pm May-Sep)

Babylon Beach MEDITERRANEAN €€€

14 ✖ MAP P86, B3

With a fashionable vibe and beanbags and wooden tables by the waves, this happening bar-restaurant is your best bet for a beachside bite or cocktail. Most produce is organically sourced in Ibiza, some from Babylon Beach's own farm. Choose between the relaxed *chiringuito* (beach bar) or the smarter restaurant. It's 1km northeast of Santa Eulària, just off the coast road. (📞971 33 21 81; www.babylonbeachbar.com; Carrer Bartomeu Tur Clapes 20; mains €19-26; ⏱10am-8pm Apr-Oct; 📶)

El Naranjo SEAFOOD, INTERNATIONAL €€

15 ✖ MAP P86, C5

Hidden away from the town bustle, 'The Orange Tree' sits on a pretty, quiet courtyard draped in bougainvillea. The fish (such as sea bass in a salt crust) is always fresh and cooked to retain all its juices, while other Spanish-international offerings include seafood spaghetti and entrecôte in three-pepper sauce. The three-course *menú del día* (daily set menu; €11) is a steal. (📞971 33 03 24; www.facebook.com/elnaranjoibiza; Carrer Sant Josep 31; mains €9-17; ⏱1-4pm & 7pm-midnight Tue-Sun; 📶)

El Bacaro ITALIAN €€

16 ✖ MAP P86, D5

A reliable, welcoming and theatrically styled Italian restaurant in Santa Eulària's marina, plating up the best pizza and calzone in town, plus good seafood and pasta and a few regional dishes from Venice, the owner's home town. It also does brunch-time bruschetta, juices, fruit salads and more, and you can dine on the gorgeous seafront terrace (book ahead). (📞971 33 19 43; www.facebook.com/elbacaroibiza; Carrer Isidor Macabich 35; mains €12-20; ⏱noon-midnight Mar–mid-Jan)

Chirincana SPANISH, INTERNATIONAL €€

17 ✖ MAP P86, C3

A boho-feel beach shack on sandy Cala Martina, 4.5km northeast of Santa Eulària, that turns out pizzas, tapas and tasty vegetarian bites, including local-veg salads, hummus platters and falafel combos. Also hosts live music (usually

Santa's Street of Restaurants

Just off the northeast side of Plaça d'Espanya you'll find Santa Eulària's famous 'street of restaurants'. Pedestrianised **Carrer Sant Vicent** has over a dozen places to eat, ranging from cafes, simple tapas bars and world-wandering eateries to upmarket restaurants such as **Es Terral**.

on Wednesday) and dance-on-the-beach DJ parties. Keep up to speed with its Facebook page. (☎971 93 54 03; www.facebook.com/chirincanaibiza; Avinguda Punta Arabí, Cala Martina; dishes €12-18; ⏱9am-1am Jun-Sep, 10am-1am May & Oct; 🖬)

Drinking

Guaraná   CLUB

18 📍 MAP P86, D5

Opening on to a terrace right by the marina, Santa Eulària's only club is a classy option away from the Ibiza–Sant Rafel–Sant Antoni circuit. Local DJs man the decks, spinning deep house, and there's often live music. Check

the Facebook page for upcoming events. (www.facebook.com/guaranaibiza; Passeig Marítim; ⏱8pm-6am May-Oct)

Royalty   BAR, CAFE

19 📍 MAP P86, C5

This age-old drinking institution enjoys a prime town-centre corner plot between palms, overlooking the Passeig de s'Alamera. It's a popular spot to swig a beer or sip a coffee and watch the world go by. Prices are very moderate, with *combinados* (spirit and mixer) at around €6.50, fuss-free tapas lining the bar and a three-course *menú del día* for €16. (www.facebook.com/royaltyibiza; Carrer Sant Jaume 51; ⏱7.30am-1am May-Oct, to 11pm Nov-Apr)

Shopping

Luz de Luna   FASHION & ACCESSORIES

20 🔒 MAP P86, C6

Just back from the seafront, Santa Eulària's most stylish boutique stocks flowing and fitted island-chic dresses in silk and cotton, boho bags, quirky jewellery and feather-embellished weaved bags, featuring plenty of bright prints, bold patterns and Ibizan brands. (☎661 526870; www.facebook.com/Luzdelunaibiza; Carrer Mariano Riquer Wallis 7A; ⏱10am-1.30pm & 6-9pm Mon-Fri, 10am-2pm Sat)

Can Cosmi

Long-standing, no-nonsense **Can Cosmi** (☎971 80 73 15; http://cancosmi.com; Carrer Sant Jaume 44; tapas €5-9, mains €10-20; ⏱7am-1am), on Santa's palm-dotted central boulevard, serves all-day inexpensive tapas and simple breakfasts, as well as a full-blown Spanish menu (paella, grilled meats, fresh fish). It's said to have invented the famous Ibizan *tostada* (toasted baguette with ripe tomato topping). There's a set lunch menu (€11), plus a good-value tapas-tasting deal (six for €27).

Hippy Market Punta Arabí

Hippy Market Punta Arabí

MARKET

21 🔒 MAP P86, C3

Ibiza's original hippy market gets cracking on Wednesdays (in season), with live music and drumming, artisan stalls flogging gorgeous Ibiza-made crafts, plus other boho island buys ranging from dreamcatchers to Adlib fashion. It's one of the island's largest markets, with paella, pizza and other food and drink stalls, and there's a special kids' corner dedicated to activities such as flower-crown-making.

Punta Arabí is 5km northeast of Santa Eulària. (www.hippymarket. info; Punta Arabí; ⏱10am-6pm Wed Apr-Oct)

Polen

FOOD & DRINKS

22 🔒 MAP P86, D5

This stylish deli sells all kinds of gourmet produce from Ibiza, including honey and salt, as well as fair-trade and organic foodstuffs such as granola, tea and wine. (✆634 843374; www.facebook.com/ polen.ibiza; Carrer Sant Llorenç 14; ⏱10am-2pm & 5-8.30pm Mon-Fri, 10am-2pm Sat)

Explore ◈

North & Interior Ibiza

The least-populated and most rustic part of the island, northern Ibiza has a boho, off-grid vibe thanks to its strong hippy heritage and spectacular remote landscapes. This is a region of forested hills, twisting backroads, timeworn villages and some of Ibiza's most exquisite, secluded coves. Portinatx is the north's busiest resort and Sant Joan offers a slice of low-key Ibizan life, while Sant Carles, Sant Llorenç and Santa Gertrudis also await discovery.

Beach lovers will want to hit naturally beautiful northern sands such as Benirràs, Aigües Blanques or Cala d'en Serra; lunch shoreside on fresh seafood at the first two, before throwing on a mask and snorkel (visibility often tops 30m).

Inland, allow time to explore delightful Santa Gertrudis, where there's a wealth of boutiques, bars, cafes and restaurants. And seek out little Sant Llorenç, with its sparkling-white fortified church and inspiring eateries.

Getting There & Around

🚌 L16 Santa Eulària–Sant Carles (four to 12 daily, more on Saturday).

🚌 L20 Ibiza Town–Sant Llorenç–Sant Joan (one to five daily, no Sunday service November to April); L20A continues to Portinatx.

🚌 L25 Ibiza Town–Santa Gertrudis–Sant Miquel (five to 10 daily Monday to Saturday).

North & Interior Ibiza Map on p104

Benirràs (p99) PAWEL KAZMIERCZAK/SHUTTERSTOCK ©

Top Experience 📷
Shop Sant Carles de Peralta's Hippy Market

A quiet, unhurried village, 6km northeast of Santa Eulària, pretty Sant Carles de Peralta has been pulling in bohemian travellers since the 1960s. Lead was mined in the region from Roman times until the early 20th century, but today it's tourism that fires the local economy. Come for the massive, world-famous Las Dalias hippy market and the elegant 18th-century church.

◎ MAP P104, E3

Bus L16 links Sant Carles with Santa Eulària (€1.55, 10 minutes, four to 12 daily mid-May to mid-October, four to six daily mid-October to mid-May; extra buses on Saturdays).

Església de Sant Carles

Sant Carles' village **church** (Plaça de l'Església; ⏰hours vary) is a striking whitewashed 18th-century building, with an impressive arcaded, wood-beamed entrance porch and a simple single-nave interior. Today's peaceful scene belies a traumatic past: in 1936, during the Spanish Civil War, Republican forces hanged both the village priest and his father from the carob tree that still stands outside the church. American author Elliot Paul's account of the incident in his *Life and Death of a Spanish Town* tells that the father and son were killed after taking shots at Republican troops from the belfry.

Es Trull de Ca n'Andreu

A fine example of an Ibizan *casament* (farmhouse), 17th-century **Es Trull de Ca n'Andreu** (⏰Mar-Oct, hours vary) is a blinding-white structure of tiny windows, overflowing bougainvillea and low timbered roofs. 'Es Trull' refers to the house's massive 18th-century olive press, which you'll find in the traditional kitchen. Ibizan farming tools, musical instruments and handmade baskets are also exhibited, and local wines and *hierbas* liquor are available for purchase. It's just beyond the southern edge of Sant Carles (signposted).

Las Dalias

Saturdays see little Sant Carles spring to life for its famed **Las Dalias** (www.lasdalias.es; Carretera Santa Eulària-Sant Carles Km 12; ⏰10am-8pm Sat year-round, plus 7pm-1am Mon & Tue Jun-Sep & Sun Aug; pictured) hippy market: an Ibizan wonderland of rainbow throws, Indian beads, feathered bikinis, flower crowns, books, ethnic CDs, bongo drums, paintings, incense, hats and hand-embroidered bags. It's as much about the scene as the shopping, with juice bars, food stalls, massages, fortune telling, live music and island-chic fashion everywhere.

★ Top Tips

○ Bring your swimming gear: there are several spectacular beaches within easy reach of Sant Carles, including Cala Mastella (p87) and Cala Boix (p87).

○ Saturdays are always very busy in Sant Carles, thanks to the huge Las Dalias hippy market.

○ For a quieter market experience, visit on summer weeknights.

✗ Take a Break

An essential Sant Carles stop, Bar Anita (p115) is one of the island's original hippy hang-outs (the art on its walls is said to have been donated to clear bar tabs); make sure you try the speciality house *hierbas* liquor, and a snack from the local-style menu.

Alternatively, rustic Cas Pagès (p111) serves up authentic, inexpensive Ibizan cooking and grilled meats.

Top Experience 📷
Catch a Fabulous Sunrise on the Northern Beaches

Ibiza has more than 30 coves, and the northern beaches of Benirràs, Aigües Blanques and Cala d'en Serra are three of the finest. Benirràs is infused with a distinctly hippy identity rooted in the wild happenings of the 1960s; nudist Aigües Blanques is a boho favourite with fabulous Balearic sunrises; and Cala d'en Serra, (just) accessible by car, feels like a real discovery.

◎ MAP P104

Bus L23: Ibiza Town–Benirràs (€2.95, 45 minutes, three to five daily June to September). L16C: Santa Eulària–Aigües Blanques (€2.50, 20 minutes, four daily Monday to Saturday June to mid-October).

Benirràs

Reached by two dramatic serpentine roads, the distant, silvery northern bay of **Benirràs** (Map p104, C2) has high forested cliffs, a trio of bar-restaurants, and sunbeds with jade-hued umbrellas to rent. It's a dreamy location for sunset. On Sundays there's always an assembly of drummers banging out a salutation to the sinking sun. The curiously shaped island at the mouth of the bay is Cap Bernat – it's said to resemble a praying nun, the Carthaginian goddess Tanit, or even the Sphinx. Benirràs is 4km northeast of Port de Sant Miquel. Bus L23 runs to/from Ibiza Town (three to five daily June to September).

Aigües Blanques

This exposed, east-facing gold-sand **beach** (Map p104, E2) gets its name (White Waters) from the surf, which whips up here in strong winds. Most of the year things are very tranquil, and the scenery is stunning, with several sandy bays divided by crumbling cliffs. This is an official nudist beach, popular with Ibiza's hippy community. It's the perfect spot to witness a sunrise over the Mediterranean and has a couple of *chiringuitos* (beach bars). It's 4km northeast of Sant Carles; park and walk 10 (steep) minutes down. Bus L16C links Santa Eulària with Aigües Blanques (four daily Monday to Saturday June to mid-October).

Cala d'en Serra

This sheltered **bay** (Map p104, E1; pictured), 2.5km east of Portinatx, is one of the island's prettiest, reached by a spectacular road offering a succession of vistas over azure water below (though the road is in terrible condition). A collection of fishers' shacks dots the small sandy beach, sadly somewhat disfigured by a long-abandoned hotel just above. You can swim (or scramble over rocks) to a second deserted cove just south for secluded sunbathing. Cala d'en Serra's much-loved *chiringuito* was closed indefinitely at the time of writing.

★ Top Tips

o Benirràs gets very busy on Sundays; arrive early to snag a parking spot.

o Sun worshippers (or shade seekers): note that the high cliffs around Aigües Blanques cast a shadow over the beach in the late afternoon.

o The dirt track down to Cala d'en Serra is full of potholes; it's best to park at the top and walk around 10 minutes down (unless you have a high-clearance vehicle).

o There are no buses to Cala d'en Serra.

✗ Take a Break

The inexpensive Chiringuito Aigües Blanques (p111), at the far southern end of Aigües Blanques beach, is always busy.

For a meal near Cala d'en Serra, head west to Portinatx to savour fresh seafood combined with Japanese and Peruvian inspiration on the seaside terrace at Los Enamorados (p109).

Walking Tour 🚶

Hanging Out in Santa Gertrudis

Blink and you'll miss lively little Santa Gertrudis, 11km north of Ibiza Town. This once-sleepy whitewashed village at the island's heart is a gem. Wander its compact core to uncover art-and-craft galleries, antiques shops, chic boutiques, low-lying homes and great cafe-bars around pedestrianised Plaça de l'Església. For a teensy village, it has some exceptional restaurants.

Walk Facts

Start Carrer Venda de Sa Picassa Bajos

Finish Plaça de l'Església

Length 1km

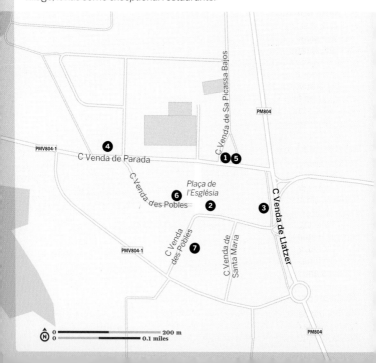

❶ A Stylish Start

Musset (☎971 19 76 71; www.facebook.com/MussetSantaGertrudis; Carrer Venda de Sa Picassa Bajos; dishes €6-17; ⏱9am-midnight, closed 1 week early Jan; 🕸🍴) is a chic all-year cafe-restaurant with elegant turquoise-tastic decor and a glass floor showcasing a terracotta seabed sculpture. The à la carte breakfasts (served until a very-Ibizan 1.30pm) are excellent.

❷ Village Church

The 18th-century **Església de Santa Gertrudis** (Plaça de l'Església; ⏱hours vary) has an impressive facade, its small windows and 19th-century bell tower picked out with yellow paint. The largely plain interior is embellished with a few decorative touches, including oranges and figs, a nod to Santa Gertrudis' status as Ibiza's principal fruit-growing village.

❸ Healthy Lunch

Stylish, always-a-hit **Wild Beets** (☎971 19 78 70; http://wildbeets.com; Carrer Venda de Llatzer 9; mains €9-16; ⏱9am-11pm Apr-Oct, 10am-5pm Nov-Mar; 🕸🍴) continues to cause a stir, offering a gloriously creative, organic vegan menu with plenty of raw-food, gluten-free and wild-bowl options. Expect generous portions and outstanding salads.

❹ Book Browsing

West of the centre, **Libro Azul** (www.libro-azul-ibiza.com; Carrer Venda de Parada 21; ⏱10.30am-2pm Mon & Sat, 10.30am-2pm & 5-8pm Tue-Fri) has a good stock of tomes about Ibiza's culture, history and nature, as well as art and design coffee-table books, photography titles and literature in various languages. It often hosts readings and book launches.

❺ Fashion Hunt

Its name inspired by the sustainable international community of Auroville in southern India, boutique **Aurobelle** (☎971 19 76 44; https://aurobelle.com; Carrer Venda de Parada 6; ⏱10am-10pm Mon-Sat, 11am-4pm & 6-10pm Sun) is all about the hippy-chic creations of German designer Jane Naeke. Most of her garments are responsibly procured from small-scale Indian artisans, with fabrics decorated using Rajasthani-style hand-block printing.

❻ Evening Drinks

Santa Gertrudis' most famous hang-out, **Bar Costa** (☎971 19 70 21; Plaça de l'Església 11; ⏱8am-1am Wed-Mon, closed 1 month in winter, often Feb) is plastered with original paintings throughout its cavernous interior. It's great for a relaxed drink and simple tapas (€3 to €9).

❼ Dine in Style

Deservedly one of Ibiza's most popular Italian restaurants, **Macao Cafe** (☎971 19 78 35; www.facebook.com/macaocafesg; Carrer Venda des Pobles 8; mains €14-33; ⏱7.30pm-midnight Apr-Sep; 🕸) spills out onto a gorgeous tree-shaded summer terrace with white-cloth tables. It's pricey but worth the splurge.

Driving Tour 🚙

Off-the-Beaten-Track Coves

Even at the peak of the August high season, some of the coves sweeping across northern Ibiza remain almost deserted. Most of these require a little effort to reach: you'll often have to drive a winding road, then walk a while. Your reward is a sense of wild isolation, with just the majesty of the coastal landscape to marvel at.

Trip Facts

Start Pou des Lleó
Finish Cala d'Aubarca
Length 50km

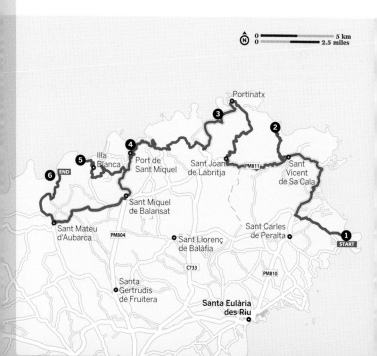

❶ Pou des Lleó

A small pebble-and-sand **bay** ringed by red cliffs and fishing huts, Pou des Lleó is 5km east of Sant Carles. You can drive right up to the shore, and during summer (late May to September) there's a *chiringuito* for snacks and drinks. Also here is **Restaurante Salvadó** (p112), an old-school spot specialising in seafood.

❷ Port de Ses Caletes

From the tiny village of Sant Vicent de Sa Cala (6km east of Sant Joan), a steep, twisting road ascends a hillside before plunging to a delightfully remote pebbly **cove**, less than 100m across, where there are just a few dilapidated fishers' huts. Cliffs soar above the bay. For solitude and silence, you can't beat Port de Ses Caletes. It's 3km north of Sant Vicent.

❸ Cala Xuclar

This protected **beach** lies at the bottom of a steep, fiddly dirt track, 2km southwest of Portinatx. Once you reach the shore, its turquoise waters dazzle the eyes, overlooked by a few fishermen's huts. Bring snorkelling gear to explore the clear underwater world below. Just back from the beach, **Chiringuito Cala Xuclar** (p111) is excellent for seafood.

❹ Caló des Moltons

This divine little **cove** lies just 250m west of Port de Sant Miquel: follow the unsigned path west around the bay to reach a small sandy beach with wonderfully sheltered swimming and the fantastic **Chiringuito Utopía** (p110). If you continue along the same trail for another 1km, you'll come to the 18th-century **Torre des Molar** defence tower, 100m above the water.

❺ Es Portitxol

Encircled by a necklace of cliffs, this tiny, lonely and very isolated horseshoe-shaped rocky **cove** is perfect for escaping the Ibiza mayhem. Most of the year there's no one here, except the odd fisherman (fishers' huts fringe the back of the bay). It's a 20-minute walk northwest of the Illa Blanca *urbanización* (residential area), 5km northwest of Sant Miquel.

❻ Cala d'Aubarca

This giant bite-shaped **bay** spans around 3km, and its sheer scale never fails to impress. It's signposted 2km north of Sant Mateu; a rough dirt track leads 2km further north to wooded cliffs high above the bay. There's no beach; park and hike down to the shoreline (around 20 minutes).

North & Interior Ibiza

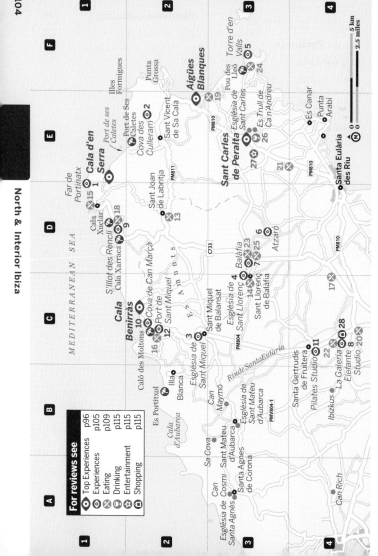

For reviews see

Top Experiences	p96
Experiences	p105
Eating	p109
Drinking	p115
Entertainment	p115
Shopping	p115

MEDITERRANEAN SEA

Far de Portinatx

Illes Formigues

Punta Grossa

Cala d'en Serra 1

Port de ses Caletes

Port de Ses Caletes 2
Cova des Culleram

Aigües Blanques 19

Torre d'en Valls

Pou des Lleó 24
Es Trull de Ca n'Andreu 26

Sant Carles de Peralta

Església de Sant Carles 27

Sant Vicent de Sa Cala

Sant Joan de Labritja

Cala Xuclar 15
Cala Xarraca 9 18

S'Illot des Renclí

Cala Benirràs 10
Cova de Can Marçà
Port de Sant Miquel 12 16

Cala de Molton

Es Portixol

Illa Blanca

Cala d'Aubarca

Església de Sant Miquel 3

Sant Miquel de Balansat

Església de Balàfia 4
Sant Llorenç 23 14 25
Sant Llorenç de Balàfia 7
Atzaró 6

Can Maymó

Església de Sant Mateu d'Aubarca

Riu de Santa Eulària

Santa Gertrudis de Fruitera

Pilates Studio 11
La Galeria 22
Elefante 8 28
Studio 20

Ibizkus

Sa Cova

Santa Agnès de Corona

Can Cosmi
Església de Santa Agnès

Can Rich

Es Canar

Punta Arabí

Santa Eulària des Riu

5 km
2.5 miles

Experiences

Far de Portinatx
LIGHTHOUSE

1  MAP P104, D1

There are many lighthouses sprinkled around the Balearics, but this majestic candy-striped structure is the tallest: 52m high, with a 2.25m-wide lantern. From Platja Es Port (with parking) at the northeast tip of Portinatx, a beautiful semi-marked path tracks northeast to the lighthouse. It follows rugged cliffs high above the sea, dipping past rocky bays and through patches of pine forest. On clear days you can see as far as southern Mallorca. Allow a leisurely hour there and back. (Far des Moscarter)

Cova des Culleram
CAVE

2  MAP P104, E2

You'll need your imagination to fully appreciate this modest-looking cave, 5km northwest of Cala de Sant Vicent. Consisting of a few small chambers, it isn't visually impressive, but it does form a vital part of Ibiza's cultural legacy. The cave was an important Carthaginian place of worship until the 2nd century BC – around 600 terracotta images of the fertility and fortune goddess Tanit have been found here. Reflecting Ibiza's hippy-spiritual side, many visitors still leave offerings to Tanit. (Santuari Púnic des Culleram; admission free; ⏱10am-1.30pm)

Cova de Can Marçà (p108)

Església de Sant Miquel

CHURCH

3 ◉ MAP P104, C2

Sant Miquel's shimmering-white 14th-century church-fortress sits atop a low-rise hill, on the site of a ruined Moorish-era farmstead. The restored early-17th-century frescoes in its Capella de Benirràs are a swirl of flowers and twisting vines in cream, black and earthy red. Wander around the back of the church to best appreciate its fortifications. Every Thursday from June to September, there's traditional **island dancing** – *ball pagès*

– on the pretty patio at 6.15pm (adult/child €5/3). (Puig de Missa; ⏲dawn-dusk, hours vary)

Església de Sant Llorenç

CHURCH

4 ◉ MAP P104, C3

Overlooking Sant Llorenç, this luminous-white, typically Ibizan 18th-century fortress-church is one of the island's most elegant, built at a time when attacks by North African raiders were the scourge of the island. A broad porch through a single entrance arch gives way to a nave with an

Other Blissful Northern Villages

Sant Miquel de Balansat sits 4km south of Port de Sant Miquel (p108) and is one of the island's largest inland villages; it isn't a picture-postcard place, but its little hillock (once a refuge from pirates) is graced with old cottages, a boutique or two and a 14th-century fortified church. Six kilometres southwest, tiny **Sant Mateu d'Aubarca** remains one of Ibiza's most isolated villages and the focus of the region's farming community, with several local vineyards (p114), a winter wine festival (p114) and an 18th-century **church-fortress** (Map p104, B3; Carretera PMV804-1; ⏲hours vary) sporting a triple-arched front porch.

Comprising a few houses and restaurants, including **Can Cosmi** (p112), **Santa Agnès de Corona** lies hidden away in the far northwest of the island, and centres on a rustic, beautifully blanched **church** (Map p104, A3; Plaça de l'Església; ⏲hours vary), which dates from 1806 and has a gorgeous arched side-porch. The village is surrounded by thousands of almond trees, which fill the plain with pinky-white blossom in late January and early February – a spectacular sight.

Over in northeast Ibiza, 8km southwest of Sant Joan (p110), the tranquil, diminutive hamlet of **Sant Llorenç de Balàfia** extends in the shadow of a dignified 18th-century fortress-church. Drop in for its excellent restaurants and once-fortified Balàfia, 1km northeast of town.

attractive barrel-vaulted roof.
(⏱ dawn-dusk, hours vary)

Torre d'en Valls
TOWER

5 ◉ MAP P104, F3

With majestic views over the Mediterranean from a patch of volcanic rock, 1km east of Pou des Lleó (p103) beach, the 18th-century Torre d'en Valls is one of the island's best-preserved defence towers (it was restored in the 1980s following a 19th-century explosion). Ibiza's towers were manned night and day, and, if raiders were sighted, a horn was sounded or a fire lit so islanders knew to take refuge. From this tower you get a terrific perspective of Tagomago islet. (Torre de Campanitx)

Atzaró
SPA

6 ◉ MAP P104, D3

For a taste of Atzaró's rural magic, book in for a blissful spa session between hushed Mediterranean gardens at this luxurious hotel hideaway (p88). Day passes provide access to the slender spa pool, hot tub, lounge beds and hammam, with a meal included, and you can also throw in a massage (total €110). Atzaró is 2.5km east of Sant Llorenç. (☎ 971 33 88 38; www.atzaro.com; Carretera Santa Eulària-Sant Joan Km 15; day pass €45; ⏱ 10am-8pm)

Balàfia
VILLAGE

7 ◉ MAP P104, D3

Take a lane west off the C733 beside the Camí de Balàfia (p112)

Portinatx

Ringed by sparkling sea, 7km north of Sant Joan, Portinatx is the north coast's major tourist resort. Busy, yes, but it's an attractive spot (especially for families) and positively underpopulated when set against the megaresorts of Ibiza Town and the island's south. Its three blonde beaches – **S'Arenal Petit**, **S'Arenal Gran** and **Platja Es Port** – are all beautiful and lapped by aquatinted waters, though also often crowded.

restaurant, 2km northeast of Sant Llorenç, to find the once-fortified hamlet of Balàfia, where two homes have their own defence towers. Balàfia is often considered an Arabic-origin village, though the only thing definitely Arabic about the settlement is its name. There are a lot of *privado* (private) signs, but don't let these deter you from exploring its couple of lanes (which aren't private).

La Galería Elefante Studio
YOGA

8 ◉ MAP P104, C4

Regular morning and evening yoga classes to suit a variety of styles and levels, held by professional instructors in a bright, attractive studio 2km southeast of Santa Gertrudis. Drop-ins are very welcome; check the latest schedules online.

Don't miss La Galería Elefante's beautiful, community-friendly concept boutique (p115). (📞971 19 70 17; www.lagaleriaelefantestudio.com; Carretera Eivissa-Sant Miquel de Balansat Km 3.2; classes €12-15)

S'Illot des Renclí   BEACH

9 ◉ MAP P104, D1

Between Calas Xuclar and Xarraca, just a few metres north of the main coastal road, you'll find the teeny-tiny cove of S'Illot des Renclí. An inviting patch of sand folds into shallow, translucent water that's perfect for swimming, and there's also a well-regarded seafood restaurant here. Just offshore is S'Illot (the Islet) that gives the beach its name. It's 2.5km southwest of Portinatx.

Cova de Can Marçà   CAVE

10 ◉ MAP P104, C2

A signposted turn-off as you enter Port de Sant Miquel from the

DIY Mud Pack

Forget the glam spas: Ibiza has its own free natural remedies. For a simple DIY beauty treatment, mix water with the rich, muddy earth from the cliffs around bays such as **Xarraca**, **Aigües Blanques** (p99) or **Sa Caleta** (p73). Then cover yourself head-to-toe in the homemade mud pack, bake under the Ibizan sun until dry, and then dive into the sea to wash it all off.

south loops 1km northeast around a headland to these underground caverns, once a smugglers' hideaway and now dramatically illuminated by coloured lights. Forty-minute tours in various languages run roughly every 30 minutes. After resurfacing, pause for a drink on the **terrace bar** and savour the panorama of sheer cliffs and deep-blue water. (www.covadecan-marsa.com; Port de Sant Miquel; adult/child €11/7; ⏰10.30am-8pm May-Oct, 11am-5.30pm Nov-Apr)

Pilates Studio   HEALTH & FITNESS

11 ◉ MAP P104, C4

At this professional, well-equipped studio on the eastern edge of Santa Gertrudis, experienced instructors lead small-group and private classes using mat work, reformer machines, the 'tower' and the 'chair'. Personal trainers are also available for redcord and weights workouts. Book ahead. (📞610 428551; www.pilatestudioibiza.com; Carrer Venda de Llatzer 11; group class per person €20; ⏰9am-9pm Mon-Fri, 10am-2pm Sat)

Port de Sant Miquel   BEACH

12 ◉ MAP P104, C2

Originally a fishing village, 4km north of Sant Miquel de Balansat, this popular north-coast resort has a fine white-sand beach dominated by the huge concrete honeycomb of the Club San Miguel hotel. In this attractive, deep-sunk bay, you can waterski, canoe and hire snorkelling gear to explore the rocky shoreline.

Eating

Giri Café
SPANISH €€

13 ⊗ MAP P104, D2

This stunning cafe-restaurant, with an exquisitely stylish rustic-chic interior and a blissful garden, ticks all the right progressive foodie boxes: seasonal, locally sourced, sustainably produced and (mainly) organic ingredients. But does raved-about Giri deliver? It certainly does. From Iberian ham platters and rosemary-sprinkled chips to falafel burgers and salmon tartar with avocado, parsley-coriander mayo and yuzu, imaginative dishes are beautifully presented. (☏ 971 33 34 74; https://cafe.thegiri.com; Plaça d'Espanya 5, Sant Joan de Labritja; mains €11-25; ⏰ 10am-midnight Apr-Oct; 🛜🚲)

Giri Café

🕐 cafe 12.30-4.30pm year-round, closed Mon Nov-Apr & 3 weeks Jan, restaurant 8pm-midnight May-Oct, 7-11pm Tue-Sat Nov, Dec, Mar & Apr; 🛜🚲)

La Paloma
MEDITERRANEAN €€€

14 ⊗ MAP P104, C3

A mellow vibe permeates this boho-chic restaurant set amid lush gardens, just downhill from Sant Llorenç's church. The weekly-changing menu is Italian with a creative slant: pastas, risottos, homemade focaccia, herby salads with garden-grown veg, and a terrific *solomillo* (beef steak) with balsamic and thyme. The cafe serves great quiches, salads, cakes and organic smoothies on a shady, overgrown terrace. Service can be a little slow in summer, when you'll definitely need to book ahead. (☏ 971 32 55 43; http://palomaibiza.com; Sant Llorenç; mains €16-28;

Los Enamorados
INTERNATIONAL, FUSION €€€

15 ⊗ MAP P104, D1

Zingy Japanese and Peruvian flavours collide with fresh Ibizan seafood at this deliciously stylish terrace bar-restaurant, occupying a century-old boathouse on Portinatx' glittery northernmost bay. Hammocks, dangling lamps, turquoise-tiled walls and mango-yellow umbrellas create a mellow-luxe vibe, while the creative, want-to-try-everything menu meanders from avocado gazpacho and mixed ceviche to grilled sea bass wrapped in a banana

Sant Joan de Labritja

Though it remains a small, mellow village, delightful **Sant Joan** is one of northern Ibiza's main settlements (and a municipal capital). Along its charming little main street, you'll find a cluster of shops, venerable whitewashed cottages and a sprinkling of excellent cafe-restaurants with an organic leaning, including the fabulous **Giri Café** (p109). Throw in a handful of enticing hotels and Sant Joan makes the perfect base for exploring the island's beautiful north.

Geographically isolated from Ibiza's capital and with its own distinct rural character, Sant Joan has long been a popular hang-out for writers, artists and escapees. Counterculture is virtually mainstream here, and the village has played host to esoteric types ever since the days of the Bhagwan Rajneesh cult (p113) back in the 1970s.

Sant Joan's only real sight is the whitewashed **Església de Sant Joan** (Plaça de l'Església; ⏱hours vary), a slightly unusual (for Ibiza) 18th-century construction with distinctive splashes of yellow paint and a slim steeple dating from the 20th century. Its interior is very plain, with a chequered-floor nave topped by a barrel-vaulted roof.

On Sundays, Sant Joan hosts a wonderful local artisans' and **farmers' market** (⏱10am-4pm Sun), with stalls selling organic local produce alongside traditional crafts and handicrafts in the village centre.

leaf. Book ahead. (📞971 33 75 49; https://losenamoradosibiza.com; Carrer de Portinatx 103, Platja Es Port; mains €18-30; ⏱8am-12.30pm, 1-4pm & 7.30-10.30pm mid-Apr–Oct)

Chiringuito Utopía
SPANISH, SEAFOOD €€

16 ✖ MAP P104, C2

An inviting, subtly stylish little beach shack tucked into a tiny sandy bay, 250m west of Port de Sant Miquel. The friendly team serve tasty salads, cheese boards, burgers and fresh fish, and sizzle up a fab *sardinada* (sardine barbecue) on Fridays. There are daybeds for lounging, and impromptu live-music events are

sometimes held here. Cash only. (www.facebook.com/UtopiaChiringuito; Caló des Moltons, Port de Sant Miquel; dishes €10-20; ⏱10am-10pm Mon-Fri, 1-10pm Sat & Sun May-Sep)

Ses Escoles
IBIZAN €€

17 ✖ MAP P104, C4

Perched by the C733, 6km south of San Llorenç, this olive-oil estate doubles as an elegant *oleoteca* (olive-oil tasting room) serving Ibizan cheeses and cold meats, tapas and salads, grilled-meat mains and delicious vegetarian dishes (try grilled asparagus with basil oil), all cooked with the house olive oil. The atmospheric dusty-pink building is an old school. Book ahead on weekends. (Es Trull de Can Miquel Guasch; 871 87 02 29; www.canmiquelguasch.com; Carretera Eivissa-Portinatx Km 9.8; mains €10-20; 1-4pm & 7-11pm Tue-Sun)

Chiringuito Cala Xuclar
SEAFOOD, SPANISH €€

18 MAP P104, D1

Well hidden from the north-coast road, this little sand-side *chiringuito* makes a charming setting for some of the freshest fish in Ibiza, including grouper, monkfish and sea bass. It's an idyllic position, at the back of a sandy cove, though the place is tiny. Phone before 11am or text/ Whatsapp a day or two ahead for bookings. (607 233019, 679 670559; Cala Xuclar; mains €12-30; 10am-10pm Jun-Sep, to 7pm May & Oct)

Chiringuito Aigües Blanques
SPANISH €

19 MAP P104, E3

At the southern end of the golden, east-oriented Aigües Blanques (p99) beach, this laid-back spot is inexpensive and forever popular, serving tasty *bocadillos* (filled rolls), salads and other simple bites. (Aigües Blanques; dishes €6-15; 10am-10pm May-Oct)

Ama Lur
BASQUE €€€

20 MAP P104, C4

Housed in a sun-yellow *finca* (rural estate), 3km southeast of Santa Gertrudis, long-running Ama Lur is one of the island's best-regarded restaurants and often wins the Ibiza chefs' own annual 'Top Restaurant' vote. It's quite formal, specialising in exquisite upscale Basque cuisine that includes plenty of fish, seafood and interesting meat dishes, and an excellent (if expensive) wine list. Book in advance. (971 31 45 54; www.restauranteamalur.com; Carretera Eivissa-Sant Miquel Km 2.3; mains €25-36; 8pm-midnight Thu-Tue)

Cas Pagès
IBIZAN €€

21 MAP P104, E3

Hugely popular with *ibicencos*, this low-key, fine-value country restaurant specialises in island cuisine and barbecued meats – succulent pork steaks, tasty lamb chops – all well seasoned with Ibizan salt. Portions are huge, so if you aren't desperately hungry you could share, and there are good Ibizan wines. Eat on the attractive vine-shaded

Café Vista Alegre

With a lovely mural-embellished terrace that catches the morning sun, **Café Vista Alegre** (971 33 30 08; Carrer d'Eivissa 1, Sant Joan de Labritja; dishes €4-9; 8am-1am Mon-Sat, 4pm-1am Sun) is a laid-back local's local ideal for a *café con leche* and *tostada* (topped toast) early in the day, or a beer and a few simple tapas later on. It also dishes up traditional Ibizan desserts such as *flaó* (a mint-flavoured cheesecake variant).

terrace or in the charmingly rustic interior. No bookings. (✆971 31 90 29; http://caspages.es; Carretera Santa Eulària-Sant Carles Km 10; mains €13-25; ⏰1-3.30pm & 7.30-11.30pm Wed-Mon)

Can Caus
IBIZAN, GRILL €€

22 MAP P104, C4

Sourcing most of its produce from the island, this restaurant is renowned for its grilled meats – rabbit, lamb, chicken, *sobrassada* and *butifarrón* (local sausages), all sizzled to perfection and served with chips, baked potatoes or salad. Ibizan cheeses, wines and desserts are available, and there's a sociable atmosphere, with tables on a vine-shaded terrace. It's 1.5km southeast of Santa Gertrudis. (✆971 19 75 16; www.cancaus.com; Carretera Eivissa-Santa Gertrudis Km 3.5; mains €12-24; ⏰1-5pm & 8pm-midnight, closed Mon Oct-May; 👶)

Can Cosmi

Though isolated **Santa Agnès** is little more than a huddle of houses around a whitewashed church, it does have a terrific, simple bar-restaurant that's famous for its fabulous tortilla. Family-run **Can Cosmi** (Map p104; A3; Plaça de l'Església, Santa Agnès de Corona; dishes €7-15; ⏰noon-4pm & 7.30-11.30pm Wed-Mon) also does meat dishes, including tasty grilled chicken, all served with chips and salad on a church-facing terrace.

Camí de Balàfia
BARBECUE, IBIZAN €€

23 MAP P104, D3

A rustic Ibizan restaurant famous for its grilled meats, expertly cooked over charcoal. Just choose your meat and rustle up a tomato-and-onion salad and chips. Do savour one of the Ibizan desserts, best accompanied by a digestif of homemade *hierbas* liquor. (✆971 32 50 19; Carretera Eivissa-Sant Joan Km 15.4; mains €14-22; ⏰8-11.30pm Mon-Sat Apr-Oct, hours vary)

Restaurante Salvadó
SEAFOOD €€

24 MAP P104, F3

On a tiny bay 5km east of Sant Carles, this traditional-style seafood restaurant makes superb *bullit de peix* (fish stew; order ahead), served with *arròs a banda* (paella-style rice cooked in fish stock). Grilled fish, squid and cuttlefish are also available, along with a few salads and meat dishes. Some tables overlook the water. (✆669 634700, 971 18 78 79; www.facebook.com/Restaurante-salvado; Pou des Lleó; mains €12-33; ⏰1-4.30pm & 7.30-10.30pm Apr-Oct)

Es Pins
IBIZAN €€

25 MAP P104, D3

Classic, no-nonsense roadside Ibizan restaurant offering a straightforward, good-value menu. It's charmingly old school – portions are huge and the decor feels log-cabin homey. *Sofrit pagès* (country meat fry-up) is the house

Ibiza's Hippy Heritage

Northern Ibiza has been a focus for the island's hippies since the mid-1960s. With a tolerant local community and cheap farmhouses, many settled in the area. Mail could be collected at **Bar Anita** (p115) in Sant Carles, and the hippies' ranks were boosted by American draft dodgers fleeing the Vietnam War. The 1969 film *More,* which deals with heroin addiction and has a Pink Floyd soundtrack, was filmed on the island. Later, a scene developed around the Can Tiruit commune near Sant Joan, which became a centre for the charismatic Indian guru Bhagwan Shree Rajneesh (later known as Osho). Osho preached a mix of sexual liberation, Sufism and Buddhism to thousands of mainly Western devotees (combining it with a love of Rolls-Royces). Ibiza folklore tells that Osho's followers were the first to bring MDMA to the island in the 1970s.

Countercultural Northern Beaches

Ibiza's hippy heritage can be felt everywhere across the north. At nudist beach **Aigües Blanques** (p99) there's a startling view of Tagomago island, celebrated in a 1971 album by German psychedelic rock band Can. **Benirràs** (p99) beach is also steeped in countercultural history. Full-moon parties were held here for decades and, during the build-up to the Gulf War in 1991, thousands gathered to protest – the bay reverberated to the rhythmic beat of the conga and bongo, an event later named the **Day of the Drums**. The event kept growing until it was banned due to staggering numbers. Today, you can get a flavour of the occasion each Sunday, when dozens of drummers gather at Benirràs to mark the sunset.

The Trance Scene

The energy and psychedelic edge (and drugs) of the acid house scene resonated strongly in northern Ibiza, where few identified with the glitz of Ibiza's superclubs. An underground trance movement developed in the 1990s; key venues across the north included **Portinatx lighthouse** (p105), Can Punta hilltop near Sant Joan, and Las Puertas del Cielo near Santa Agnès, which held a legendary three-day party in 1999. But as these illegal raves were increasingly targeted by the authorities, the scene dissipated. It survives in patches, with legal venues such as Sant Carles' **Las Dalias** (p115) stepping in to host psy-trance parties.

Ibizan Wine

Ibiza's arid climate is not ideal for intensive viniculture, but the island has five vineyards producing high-quality wines, mostly concentrated in the northwest around the village of **Sant Mateu d'Aubarca**. Richly aromatic local reds are favoured, mostly from earthy *monastrell* and spicy *garnatxa* (*garnacha* in Spanish; grenache) grapes, along with some tempranillo, merlot and syrah. Malvasia is the main grape variety for whites and rosés. Most Ibizan farmers also cultivate a few vines to produce *vi pagès* (country wine) for casual drinking.

Winning Wineries

Ibiza's leading wineries include the award-winning, 21-hectare **Can Rich** (Map p104, A4; 971 80 33 77; http://bodegascanrich.com; Camí de Sa Vorera; tasting per person from €15; 10am-2pm Mon-Fri), in the Buscatell area, 4km west of Sant Antoni. It produces respected reds, whites and rosés, along with fine sparkling wines and olive oil. Tastings, which can be combined with tapas and brief tours, can be booked in advance.

Just northwest of Sant Mateu, family-owned **Sa Cova** (Map p104, B3; 971 18 70 46) is an important wine producer focused on reds (25,000 bottles a year); book ahead for wine-and-tapas tastings (€18).

Ibizkus (Map p104, B4; 971 19 83 44; http://ibizkus.com; Camí Vell de Sant Mateu; 10am-4pm Mon-Fri, by appointment Sat 11am-1pm), 3km from Santa Gertrudis, makes premium rosés and a few reds from old, organically cultivated and largely ungrafted vines. Whites have recently been introduced, too, and production stands at 60,000 bottles a year. Free morning tours with tastings of four wines run Monday to Friday.

Another notable island winery is **Can Maymó** (Map p104, B3; http://bodegascanmaymo.com; 11am-2pm & 4-6pm Mon-Sat, 10am-1pm Sun), 1.5km northeast of Sant Mateu, which specialises in aromatic reds and offers tours with tastings (€15).

Wine Festival

If you're in Ibiza in December, don't miss the wonderful **Festa del Vi Pagès**, Sant Mateu d'Aubarca's annual wine-harvest festival. Everyone samples the local *vi pagès* from teapot-shaped jugs.

Stock Up

Vino & Co (p79), 4.5km southwest of Ibiza Town, is an excellent wine merchant with good supplies of Ibizan wines, often available for tasting. **Ses Escoles**, 6km south Sant Llorenç, is a gorgeous pink-washed olive-oil estate that also stocks an impressive range.

special, and there are plenty of rice dishes, meaty mains and tortillas to pick from. The three-course set lunch menu is just €11. It's on the C733 opposite the turn-off to Sant Llorenç. (📞971 32 50 34; Carretera Eivissa-Sant Joan Km 14.8; mains €6-15; ⏰8am-11.30pm Thu-Tue)

Drinking

Bar Anita   BAR

26 🚌 MAP P104, E3

A timeless tavern opposite Sant Carles' church, Bar Anita has been attracting all sorts since the hippies rocked up in the 1960s. The kitchen churns out uncomplicated, great-value tapas, salads, omelettes and mains (€5 to €18). Or simply grab a drink and a chat. Don't miss the famous homemade *hierbas* liquor, blending 16 ingredients including rosemary, fennel, orange and lemon. (Ca n'Anneta; Plaça de l'Església; ⏰7.30am-1am Mon-Sat, 9am-1am Sun)

Entertainment

Las Dalias   LIVE MUSIC

27 ⭐ MAP P104, E3

This one-size-fits-all venue caters to northern Ibiza's alternative crew with psy-trance nights, a busy bar and live music (everything from blues to Afrobeat and reggae; Manu Chao played here in 2015). DJ events include Wax da Jam for funk, soul and hip-hop sounds. Las Dalias also hosts Sant Carles' much-loved Saturday hippy market (p97). It's 1km southwest of Sant Carles. (www.lasdalias.es;

Carretera Santa Eulària-Sant Carles Km 12; ⏰8am-11pm, later for events; 🔊)

Shopping

Ses Escoles   FOOD & DRINKS

It's all about gourmet olive oil at this gorgeous deli-temple, 6km south of Sant Llorenç – the house brand is organic, extra virgin and made in Ibiza. Ses Escoles (see 17 ❌ Map p104, C4) also stocks Ibizan liquor and wines (such as Can Rich, Ibizkus and Sa Cova), natural beauty products and Balearic handicrafts. Olive-grove tours may be available; enquire ahead. There's a great cafe-restaurant (p110) here, too. (Es Trull de Can Miquel Guasch; 📞871 87 02 29; www.canmiquelguasch.com; Carretera Eivissa-Portinatx Km 9.8; ⏰noon-midnight)

La Galería Elefante   CLOTHING, HOMEWARES

28 🔒 MAP P104, C4

Duck through low-slung arches to reach artfully arranged displays at this whitewashed *finca,* now transformed into a maze-like, boho-chic boutique. Rooms are crammed with Ibiza-style beachwear, floaty dresses and kaftans, scented candles, colourful homewares, artisan crafts and other trinkets gathered from all over the world, many from ecofriendly, responsible and/or community-supportive sources. (📞971 19 70 17; www.lagaleriaelefante. com; Carretera Eivissa-Sant Miquel de Balansat Km 3.2; ⏰10am-8pm, Mon-Sat)

Explore ◈
Sant Antoni de Portmany & West Ibiza

Ibiza's western coastline conceals some beautiful sandy coves, while just inland lie sprawling vineyards and charming whitewashed villages. Infamous Sant Antoni ('San An') is about as Spanish as bangers and mash, and certainly lives up to its reputation as a Brits-abroad booze-up destination, but there's still a more chilled-out scene to be found here: along Sant Antoni's Sunset Strip – home of the legendary Café del Mar – or on the smattering of beaches to the town's north and southwest.

A stroll along Sant Antoni's seafront promenade provides the perfect introduction to Ibiza's uberlively west coast. Sights are thin on the ground, but do pop into Sant Antoni's church. Then perhaps enjoy a winery tour and a spot of beach-hopping.

It's best to explore with your own wheels, but there are summer bus and/or boat connections to most west-coast beaches.

Getting There & Around

🚌 L8/L3 Ibiza Town–Sant Antoni (€2, 25 minutes, every 15 to 30 minutes).

🚌 L9 Airport–Sant Josep–Sant Antoni (€4, 30 minutes, half-hourly or hourly mid-May–mid-Oct).

🚌 There are also summer services from Sant Antoni to nearby towns/beaches.

Sant Antoni de Portmany & West Ibiza Map on p122

Sant Antoni's seafront promenade ALEX TIHONOVS/SHUTTERSTOCK ©

Top Experience
Venture Out to the Coastal Surrounds

There are some wonderful beaches near Sant Antoni. The town borders a natural harbour and reasonable beach, but there are finer options further afield. Swooping southwest, Cala Bassa is a beautiful (busy) cove with sheltered azure waters. Beyond, Platges de Comte have top sunsets and some of Ibiza's clearest seas. To the north, Calas Salada and Gració are white-sand delights.

Sant Antoni

Bus L4 from Sant Antoni to Platges de Comte (seven to 11 daily, May to October), L7 to Cala Bassa (eight to 10 daily, June to September), L34 to Cala Salada (every 15 to 30 minutes, mid-May to September) and L1 to Cala Gració (eight to 10 daily, April to October).

Platges de Comte

Occupying a low-lying headland, this dreamy cluster of three blonde-sand **coves** enjoys shallow, fabulously clear aqua waters. The beaches face directly west, making this a ridiculously popular late-afternoon spot, with hundreds gathering to watch the sun sink into the Mediterranean, often from ultra-boho-cool bar-restaurant Sunset Ashram (p127). The small southernmost bay is favoured by nudists.

Cala Bassa

Heading 9km southwest from Sant Antoni, you'll reach alluring **Cala Bassa** (Map p122, B3), a horseshoe bay of alabaster sand backed by junipers, pines and tamarind trees. It's hugely popular for its turquoise water and blissed-out beach club. Cruceros Portmany (p150) ferries operate May to October (three to six daily).

Cala Salada

It's just 5km north of Sant Antoni, but the lovely cove of **Cala Salada** (Map p122, E1; pictured) feels a continent away, with bright-blue sea washing on to white sand. The coastal environment is spectacular, with cliffs and soaring pine-clad hills sheltering the small beach and its seafood restaurant. Clamber past the row of fishers' huts to reach more peaceful **Cala Saladeta**.

Cala Gració

Within walking distance of Sant Antoni, protected **Cala Gració** (Map p122, D2) is bordered by pine woods and has a generous stretch of fine pale sand, shallow turquoise water and a bar-restaurant. It's 1km north of Caló des Moro (at the northern end of San Antoni). On its northwest side, a path leads 100m across a rocky headland to a gorgeous smaller bay, **Cala Gracioneta**, which is just 30m wide and has soft white sand and a wonderful bar-restaurant (p124).

★ Top Tips

o There's no public transport to any of these beaches from November to April.

o Summer ferries are a fun alternative to buses for reaching Cala Bassa, Platges de Comte and Cala Salada; check Cruceros Portmany (p150).

o Parking can be impossible in high season – consider public transport.

✗ Take a Break

Half the reason to visit Platges de Comte is boho-chic Sunset Ashram (p127), which has a divine, lively terrace for drinks and global food.

Cala Salada's beach restaurant is fine, but you'll dine much better at Cala Gracioneta's *chiringuito* (beach bar; p124), to the south.

Walking Tour 🥾

Bar-Hopping in San An

San An has enough bars – pubs, lounges, club-bars, megaclubs and even local bars – to drown the devil himself. The West End (p129) is a Brit-dominated territory of pubs and football-shirt-clad drinkers. The world-famous Sunset Strip has a more mellow vibe, while the beachside promenade hosts laid-back lounge-style bars. The southwest end of the bay is an increasingly popular food-and-drink destination.

Walk Facts

Start Avinguda Dr Fleming

Finish Plaça de s'Era d'en Manyà

Length 3km

❶ Beachside Beats

Enjoying a prime beachfront location, **Ibiza Rocks Bar** (www. ibizarocks.com; Avinguda Dr Fleming; ⏰10.30am-3am May-Sep) is a haven for music lovers, with acoustic performances from the likes of Pete Doherty and Ed Sheeran, and DJ sets from artists including Annie Mac and Basement Jaxx. There's always a party fever. During the day it's fun for drinks, meals (mains €8 to €12) and hearty breakfasts.

❷ Blazing Sunsets

With its horizon-facing views, glam decor and seafront terrace, **Savannah** (www.savannahibiza.com; Carrer General Balanzat; ⏰11am-3am May-Oct; 🛜) is a fine Sunset Strip pick for a cocktail or dinner with a view. The intimate back room is a red-hot party venue (it's free to get in) and has hosted DJ talent such as Roger Sanchez. Bookings require a minimum €60 spend per person.

❸ The One and Only

Ibiza's (and Spain's) most famous bar, **Café del Mar** (☎971 80 37 58; www.cafedelmaribiza.es; Carrer de Lepant 27; ⏰5pm-midnight May–mid-Oct) is an island institution and a place of pilgrimage. The seafront bar has been serving up the same mix of atmospheric electronic beats, pricey drinks (cocktails €15) and staggering sunset views since 1980, growing to include a swanky adjacent bar-restaurant and a merchandise shop.

❹ Mambo Mambo

One of the earliest Sunset Strip bars (established in 1994), **Café Mambo** (☎971 34 66 38; www. cafemamboibiza.com; Carrer Vara de Rey 3; ⏰10am-2am) is a music-geared venue with lots of preclub action, and the warm-up bar of choice for many globally famous DJs. The premises include a stylish twin-deck restaurant terrace (book ahead; minimum spend €70). Drinks are expensive (cocktails around €15); try the *sangría de cava*.

❺ Serious Ales

If you're craving real ales, a full-monty British breakfast or a Sunday roast, look no further. The welcoming Welsh-owned **Ship Inn** (www.facebook.com/ship.inn.ibiza; Plaça de s'Era d'en Manyà; ⏰10am-3am Apr-Oct) pub is very popular with punters doing the Ibiza season, so it's good for finding out what's on and picking up tips. Prices are moderate and there are DJs and bands some nights, plus sports on the screen.

Sant Antoni de Portmany & West Ibiza

For reviews see

◎ Top Experiences	p118
◎ Experiences	p123
✕ Eating	p123
✕ Drinking	p126

MEDITERRANEAN

SEA

◎ Cala Salada

◎16

PM812

Cala Gracioneta

◎14

✕6

◎ Cala Gració

◎3 Aquarium Cap Blanc

✕10

See Sant Antoni de Portmany Enlargement

Sant Antoni de Portmany

✕5

C731

E90

PM803

Can Pujol

✕9 ✕17 11

◎18

Port des Torrent

Cala Bassa ◎

Illa des Bosc

Platges de Comte ◎

◎15

Cala Codolar

▲N

0 ——— 2 km
0 ——— 1 miles

Sant Antoni de Portmany

C Lope de Vega ✕12

Caló des Moro

C Velázquez

C Alacant

C Santa Rosalia

C Soledat

C Cervantes ✕19

C Vara de Rey

C Sant Antoni

C General Balanzat

✕8 ✕9

Pg de la Mar ✕13

C Londres

PM812

Av de Portmany

C Salvador Espriu

Av Dr Fleming

◎2

C Ramón i Cajal

C de Progrés ✕4 ✕7

Església de Sant Antoni ◎1

Pg de Ses Fonts

Sant Antoni Promenade

◎20

C de Lepant

Sunset Strip

◎21

0 ——— 500 m
0 ——— 0.25 miles

Experiences

Església de Sant Antoni CHURCH

1 ◎ MAP P122, B2

There has been a church on this spot since 1305, but the existing structure dates mainly from the 17th century. You approach the church through a lovely cobbled patio, adjoined by an attractive porch. Its key features are its rectangular defence tower (cannons were once mounted here to deter pirates) and twin belfry. (Plaça de l'Església; ◎dawn-dusk, hours vary)

Sant Antoni Promenade STREET

2 ◎ MAP P122, C3

San An's extensive harbourside promenade now stretches around the entire coastline from Caló des Moro in the north to south past the Punta des Molí promontory (where there's an old windmill). One of the best sections borders S'Arenal beach and has plenty of bars. (Avinguda Dr Fleming)

Aquarium Cap Blanc AQUARIUM

3 ◎ MAP P122, D2

In a natural, former smugglers' cave, this small aquarium is home for an assortment of local marine life, including groupers, wrasse, octopuses, lobsters, moray eels and lots of starfish. Occasionally injured turtles recuperate here. There are boardwalks above the pools so you can get a close look. (☎663 945475; www.aquariumcap-blanc.com; Carretera Cala Gració;

adult/child €5/3; ◎9.30am-10pm Jun-Sep, to 6.30pm May & Oct, 10am-2pm Sat Nov-Apr)

Eating

Es Ventall IBIZAN €€

4 ✖ MAP P122, B2

A cut above most of the Sant Antoni competition, Es Ventall offers delicious updated-Ibizan dishes such as shoulder of lamb with stir-fried veg, or *bullit de peix* (fish stew) with *arròs a banda* (paella-style rice cooked in fish stock). There are fine tapas and an impressive range of paella and *fideuà* (paella-like fish-and-seafood noodle dish), too. The garden terrace, shaded by trees, is gorgeous. (☎871 77 78 39; www.restauranteesventall.com; Carrer Cervantes 22; mains €15-32; ◎1-4pm & 8pm-midnight Thu-Tue)

LONGJON/SHUTTERSTOCK ©

Natural Pau INTERNATIONAL €

5 MAP P122, E3

A tiki-like bar, dangling swings and tables spread around a palm-dotted courtyard lure you into this gorgeous, easy-going, open-air 'flexitarian' restaurant. The imaginative, health-focused menu finds inspiration in global flavours, including stuffed flatbreads, hummus platters, salads such as mozzarella-filled courgette flowers, and protein-fuelled breakfasts of scrambled eggs and *tostadas* (topped toast). After midnight it's a fun *copeteo* (drinks) spot. (☑615 807719; Carrer Bella Vista 3; dishes €6-12; ☺9.30am-2am May–mid-Oct; 🖋)

Cala Gracioneta MEDITERRANEAN €€

6 MAP P122, D2

In a hidden bay, with tables almost on the sand, this beautifully positioned beach restaurant has a slightly castaway, barefoot vibe (though prices are more banker-than backpacker-friendly). It's part of the Mambo Group – of Café Mambo (p121) fame – and is perfect for seafood, with excellent paella. It also hires out daybeds for luxe lounging, and plays top tunes. (☑971 34 83 38; www.calagracioneta.com; Cala Gracioneta; mains €14-22; ☺10am-midnight Apr-Oct, noon-6pm Thu-Mon Nov-Mar; 🛜)

Es Rebost de Can Prats IBIZAN €€

7 MAP P122, B2

Authentic family-run Ibizan restaurants are a rare breed in Sant Antoni – all the more reason to dine at Es Rebost, in the heart of town. Go for spot-on mains such as steaks, grilled fish and *arròs melós* (creamy seafood rice), or a hearty speciality *sofrit pagès* (country fry-up). The three-course set lunch menu is good value at €15. (☑971 34 62 52; www.esrebostdecanprats.com; Carrer Cervantes 4; mains €14-25; ☺1-4pm & 8pm-midnight Wed-Mon)

Illa Sa Conillera

The large, elongated island of Sa Conillera lies within the protected **Reserves Naturals des Vedrà, es Vedranell i els illots de Ponent** (http://es.balearsnatura.com), and can be seen from many points around Sant Antoni's bay. It's uninhabited, but harbours a considerable population of rabbits (the Catalan 'Illa Conillera' translates as Rabbit Island), a unique species of wall lizard and lots of cicadas. Local folklore has it that this was the birthplace of Carthaginian general Hannibal. Illa Conillera is also said to be the best source for the narcotic plant *Hyoscyamus albus* (henbane), used by pagans for ceremonies on the night of Sant Joan. The island can only be reached by private boat and landing on it is off-limits to the general public.

Skinny Kitchen

HEALTH FOOD €€

8 MAP P122, A2

On the harbour front, this massively popular rustic-chic health-food cafe is just the ticket after a jaunt around Sant Antoni. Protein bowls, low-calorie burgers, sweet-potato fries, falafel wraps and courgette with feta appear on the fitness-fired menu, featuring excellent vegan, vegetarian and gluten-free choices. A rainbow of juices includes the oh-so-appropriate Hangover Cure, with apple, carrot and ginger. (☑971 80 46 44; www.skinnykitchen.co; Passeig de la Mar 20; mains €10-15; ☺9am-11.30pm Apr-Oct; ✎)

Rita's Cantina

BREAKFAST, INTERNATIONAL €

9 ❌ MAP P122, B2

One of the most popular places in town, Rita's serves reliably great breakfasts (from fry-ups to fruit with muesli), Mexican food, Spanish favourites, crepes and baguettes, plus an array of fresh juices and smoothies, and a famously terrific club sandwich. The front terrace, facing the harbour, is always packed on sunny days, and the muralled interior has a colonial-style feel. (☑971 34 33 87; www.ritascantina.com; Passeig de la Mar; dishes €4-8.50; ☺8am-1am; ☷)

Sa Capella

SPANISH €€€

10 ❌ MAP P122, E2

Occupying an 18th-century chapel, this upmarket, highly atmospheric and romantic restaurant

Can Pujol

The slightly run-of-the mill appearance of this busy **restaurant** (Map p122, D3; ☑971 34 14 07; www.restaurantecanpujolibiza.com; Carretera Vieja a Port des Torrent; mains €24-35; ☺1-4pm & 7.30-11.30pm Thu-Tue Dec-Oct) belies the quality (and cost) of the cuisine, which features good paella, plenty of lobster dishes and fine *bullit de peix*. It's popular with Spaniards and enjoys wonderful sunset views over the Mediterranean from its shoreside position, 4km southwest of Sant Antoni.

proves equally popular with Ibiza's old-money elite and the DJ set. Meat dishes such as suckling pig, lamb chops and rib-eye steak are elegantly cooked and presented (there's little for vegetarians), and the wine list is suitably extensive. It's 1.5km northeast of town. (☑971 34 00 57; www.facebook.com/sacapella.ibiza; Carretera Sant Antoni-Santa Agnès Km 0.5; mains €22-28; ☺8.30pm-midnight mid-Apr–mid-Oct)

Relish

INTERNATIONAL €

11 ❌ MAP P122, D3

With sea views through arches from its terrace, this laid-back lounge-restaurant does beautifully prepared globetrotting dishes such as pesto pasta, goat's-cheese salad, a selection of burgers and avocado-

Sunset Ashram

and-grilled-halloumi bruschetta, all at sensible prices. There's also a pool bar, along with real-deal Sunday roasts. Find it at the southwest end of Sant Antoni's bay (4km from the centre). (☎971 34 59 13; www. relishrestaurantibiza.com; Carrer Rioja 13, Cala de Bou; mains €10-12; ☺10am-11.30pm May–mid-Oct; ⏏)

Villa Manchega
SPANISH €€

12 🍴 MAP P122, A1

If you fancy sidestepping the Brits-abroad crowds, seek out this low-key, local restaurant turning out a straightforward menu of tapas, rice dishes, meat and fish mains (try a fisherman's platter, €33 for two people), and a simple kids' selection. It's 1km north of the harbour front. (☎971 34 62 53; www.villamanchega. com; Avinguda Isidor Macabich 19; mains €9-16; ☺noon-midnight; 👶)

Villa Mercedes
MEDITERRANEAN, SPANISH €€€

13 🍴 MAP P122, B2

Set in gorgeous gardens, this graceful 1901 Ibizan mansion overlooks the marina and offers upscale Spanish-Mediterranean cooking, from grilled vegetables and Iberian ham to local catch of the day and a two-person rib-eye steak with island-grown potatoes. There are also cocktails, some good Spanish wine picks and live music, including flamenco, almost every day. (☎971 34 85 43; www. villamercedesibiza.com; Passeig de la Mar; mains €23-34; ☺6pm-2am May-Sep, 1pm-midnight Oct-Dec)

Drinking

Hostal La Torre
BAR

14 🍺 MAP P122, D1

Big international names such as DJ Harvey join resident DJs for daily in-season sessions at this clifftop, sea-view, in-the-know terrace bar-restaurant renowned for its laid-back, old-Ibiza vibe. It's a magical sunset spot, with tables across the hillside and light bouncing off the glassy Mediterranean. Try a Balearic Spritz (gin, vermouth, passion fruit and cava) or any other fabulously creative cocktail.

Breakfast runs until 12.30pm and sometimes later (very Ibiza!), and there are tasty tapas (€9 to €16) plus elegant mains (€18 to €26) ranging from fish of the day to rack of lamb with couscous. It's also a boho-chic hotel featuring stylishly stripped-back rooms dressed in soothing whites and distressed wood. (☎971 34 22 71; www.lator-reibiza.com; Cap Negret; ⏰8am-1am)

Sunset Ashram
BAR

15 🚇 MAP P122, A3

One of Ibiza's most popular sunset hang-outs, this boho-bliss bar-restaurant sits between blonde beaches and turquoise-tinted waves. DJs, including artists such as Jon Sa Trinxa, spin their magic daily in season. It's fab for drinks and Spanish-Asian-international bites (€15 to €32), though the kitchen sometimes struggles to cope with summer crowds. Book 'terrace' tables, or order and scramble for a perch. (☎661 347222; www.sunsetashram.com; Platges de Comte; ⏰10am-8pm Apr & May, to 2am Jun-Oct)

Pikes
BAR

16 🚇 MAP P122, F2

A legendary rural hotel that's hosted the likes of Freddie Mercury, Grace Jones and Bon Jovi (and is where Wham! filmed its 'Club Tropicana' video), the Ibiza Rocks team has injected a dose of 21st-century energy into the 15th-century farmhouse – now Pikes is once again one of Ibiza's coolest hang-outs.

The line-ups are fantastic, with DJ Harvey resident in 2017 and appearances from the likes of Greg Wilson and Crazy P, as well as after-parties, gigs, flamenco shows and Sunday lunches. Pikes is simply a great place to party, with huge open-air terraces, a karaoke room and an intimate dance floor. Rooms cost from €270. (https://pikesibiza.com; Camí de Sa Vorera; ⏰May-Oct; 📶)

Electronic Mecca

San An has long been the 'entry-level' point for young Brits in Ibiza. As the rest of the island goes increasingly upmarket, the town remains (almost) as down to earth as ever, retaining an undeniable edge and energy. It's a place where underground music finds a home and wannabe DJs get the opportunity to deliver in backstreet bars.

Backtrack to 1987, and all the main players who initiated the acid-house scene were holidaying in San An. Four soul boys from London – Danny Rampling, Paul Oakenfold, Nicky Holloway and Johnny Walker – found inspiration at bars in the town, discovered ecstasy and raved to DJ Alfredo's Balearic Beats under the stars across the island at **Amnesia** (p57).

José Padilla and his eclectic, emotionally provocative sets at **Café del Mar** (p121) in the '80s and '90s really put San An on the map. A unique chill-out scene developed around Padilla's cinematic, largely electronic sets, inspiring musicians around the globe.

Sant Antoni de Portmany & West Ibiza Drinking

Kumharas

BAR

17 MAP P122, D3

On the southwest side of the bay, you can eat, drink and soak up the final rays at boho-cool Kumharas, with its hippy market, ethnic beats, shisha pipes, live music, fire shows and Asian-infused food (mains €13 to €21). Arrive early to grab a sunset-view lounge table. It's best to book for dinner; the kitchen

Sunset Strip

Sant Antoni's Sunset Strip of chill-out bars showcases the more relaxed side to Ibiza's most notorious resort. For years, this rocky coastline was the forgotten back end of town, but today it's lined with a string of elegant terrace-bars that come into their own as the sun sinks. A refurbished **promenade** (p123) links the various sections, which stretch for 1km between Carrer General Balanzat at the south end and the little bay of Caló des Moro to the north.

Mellow Beginnings

Until 1993 there was only one bar, **Café del Mar** (p121), where pioneer resident DJ José Padilla spun vinyl and sold mixtapes to a small, well-informed bunch of music lovers, mainly from the UK. British DJ Phil Mison later took to the helm, continuing the mellow vibe. **Café Mambo** (p121) opened in 1994, and by 2000 there was a scattering of similar bars along the coast.

Today's Strip

Café del Mar and Café Mambo remain the best-known venues, attracting big crowds – thousands gather here in high season, when the BBC's Radio One bounces live DJ events back to the UK, TV crews broadcast live shows and webcams beam the scene around the world. The commercialism is relentless, with many bars stocking branded merchandise.

The sunset hype has exploded in the last decade or so, and you'll now have to book a table for dinner (with a minimum spend of at least €60 per person) to secure a space at the main bars. Many people bring their own drinks, find a patch on the rocks and tune into their DJ of choice rather than pay the bars' inflated drinks prices. The sunset remains the same and, when that giant fireball starts to dip into the Mediterranean to a soundtrack of electronic beats, the spectacle is still quite something.

Don't bother bringing your bikini though: you'll have to scramble over sharp rocks for a dip along most of this coastline. The one spot with easy access is **Caló des Moro**.

opens from 7pm. (www.kumharas.
org; Carrer de Lugo 2, Cala de Bou;
⏰11am-2am Easter–mid-Oct; 📱)

Rooftop Nine ROOFTOP BAR

18 🚇 MAP P122, D3

Launched in 2016, this sleek,
360-degree-view rooftop hotel
lounge (part of the Ibiza Rocks
party empire) is one of Sant
Antoni's favourite sunset hang-
outs for its sky-high cocktail bar,
open-air infinity pool and quality
chill-out DJ sets from stars such as
José Padilla. Entry is usually free,
but there's a minimum daytime
spend for stylish sun loungers.
(www.ibizarocks.com; Sol House Mixed
By Ibiza Rocks, Carrer Granada 3-7, Cala
Pinet; ⏰11am-midnight Apr-Oct)

Ibiza Rocks Hotel CLUB

19 🚇 MAP P122, B1

Ibiza does indeed rock at this
party hotel hosting the top gigs on
the island – Dizzee Rascal, Sean
Paul, Clean Bandit, The Prodigy,
Stormzy and Arctic Monkeys have
all starred here. Bands perform
in the middle of the hotel, which
also gets packed for pool parties,
famously headlined by Craig David
in 2017 and 2018. Check line-ups
and prices online. (www.ibizarocks.
com; Carrer Cervantes 27; ⏰May-Oct)

Plastik BAR, CLUB

20 🚇 MAP P122, C2

Right by the Egg roundabout,
Plastik is one of the best club-bars

West End

Sant Antoni's prime (some
would say primeval) bar
enclave is the West End, a
cluster of streets around Carrer de Santa Agnès in the town
centre. It's home to dozens of
pubs, many British-owned and
virtually all of them British-
geared. Don't expect to bump
into many *ibicencos* here, or
for waiters to speak any Spanish. Drinks are inexpensive,
though the drunkenness, teen-
age antics and leery behaviour
won't be everyone's cup of tea.

in Sant Antoni, with quality DJs,
an intimate dance floor and lots
of pre-parties for the megaclubs.
It's unpretentious and draws a
young, loyal British crowd. (www.
plastikibiza.com; Avinguda Dr Fleming
5; ⏰8pm-4am May–mid-Oct)

Es Paradis CLUB

21 🚇 MAP P122, C2

Long-running Es Paradis is one
of the prettiest of Ibiza's macro-
clubs, with loads of marble,
greenery and a glass-pyramid roof
that defines the San An skyline. Go
for the fountains, outdoor feel, fantastic sound system and infamous
water parties (Fridays). Queues
can be enormous, so arrive early.
(www.esparadis.com; Carrer Salvador
Espriu 2; admission €25-50; ⏰11pm-
6am May-Oct)

Explore ✦

Formentera

The 20km-long island of Formentera (population 12,120) is a beautifully pure, get-away-from-it-all escape. The pace of life is blissfully languid, designed for lazy days on some of Europe's most exquisite beaches, where frost-white sand is smoothed by water in unbelievable shades of azure, turquoise and lapis lazuli. Tourism here is tightly tied to environmental ethics; there are few sights and little nightlife. Ask people what they've done for the week and they'll grin: 'Nothing; it was awesome.'

Breeze into your Formentera stay with boutique-browsing in the pretty island 'capital' Sant Francesc Xavier, with its whitewashed fortress-church. Then make for bleach-blonde sands.

Over on southeastern Formentera, La Mola peninsula hosts the famous 19th-century Far de Sa Mola. From here it's an easy backtrack to Platja de Migjorn, where beach bars and seafood restaurants abound.

Getting There & Around

⚓ Services between Ibiza Town and Formentera's La Savina include the following: Aquabus, Baleària, Mediterránea Pitiusa and Trasmapi. Departures every 20 to 30 minutes May to October (fewer November to April). Day-trip boats run from resorts, Sant Antoni and Santa Eulària in Ibiza.

✈ No airport.

Formentera Map on p134

Formentera coast PLACKATHY/SHUTTERSTOCK ©

Top Experience 📷
Pack an Umbrella for the Trucador Beaches

With sugar-white sands and perfectly turquoise water, the astonishingly beautiful, pencil-slim Trucador Peninsula rivals the world's finest beaches. Dreamy Platja Illetes slinks along the west side; on the east coast (just a few steps away) is equally gorgeous Platja Llevant. In high season, these back-to-back twin beaches get very busy, but they're still an essential Formentera experience.

Trucador Peninsula

◎ MAP P134, B1

Bus L7 from La Savina to Platja Illetes and Platja de Migjorn.

Boat From La Savina to Platja Illetes and Espalmador.

Platja Illetes

Forming the western section of the peninsula, stunning Platja Illetes (pictured) is as close a vision of the Caribbean (minus the coconut trees) as you could imagine in Europe, with blinding-white sand and translucent turquoise waters. You may never want to leave. Just offshore are the two small *illetes* (islets), **Pouet** and **Rodona**, that give the beach its name. In high season, expect lots of day trippers from Ibiza.

Platja Llevant

Through the steep sand dunes on the eastern side of the peninsula, Platja Llevant is a divine, **undeveloped beach**. The powdery sand is so white that it dazzles your eyes, and the aqua water is fantastically clear. It's also very shallow, so safe for children, and the sea warms to bathtub temperatures on summer days. There can be strong winds here; keep an eye out for warning flags.

Es Pas

The northerly tip of Formentera, Es Pas (the Crossing) is a magical place where the beaches of Llevant and Illetes combine and form a (submerged) 300m-long **sandbar** that stretches north across to the island of Espalmador. There are usually people making their way over, holding their belongings over their heads, when the sea is calm (take care with currents).

Espalmador

A low-slung, uninhabited island of dunes and sandstone off the northernmost tip of Formentera, Espalmador has a beautiful crescent-shaped beach of silky blonde sand, **Platja de S'Alga**, lapped by shallow sea. There's a natural mud pond just north of the beach, though it can dry up in summer.

★ Top Tips

o The Trucador Peninsula is part of the protected Parc Natural de Ses Salines (p67), so avoid roped-off areas and use boardwalks; admission is €6/4 for cars/motorbikes.

o Restaurants here are pricey and packed in summer, so consider bringing your own supplies.

o There's almost no natural shade on the peninsula. Umbrellas and loungers can be rented, but it's best to bring your own.

o Bus L7 runs from La Savina to Platja Illetes May to mid-October; boats shuttle from La Savina to Platja Illetes and Espalmador.

✕ Take a Break

At the southern end of Platja Illetes, Es Molí de Sal (p138) is an ancient windmill that used to pump seawater into the nearby salt pans. Today it's one of Formentera's top seafood restaurants.

Over on Platja Llevant there's Restaurante Tanga (p139).

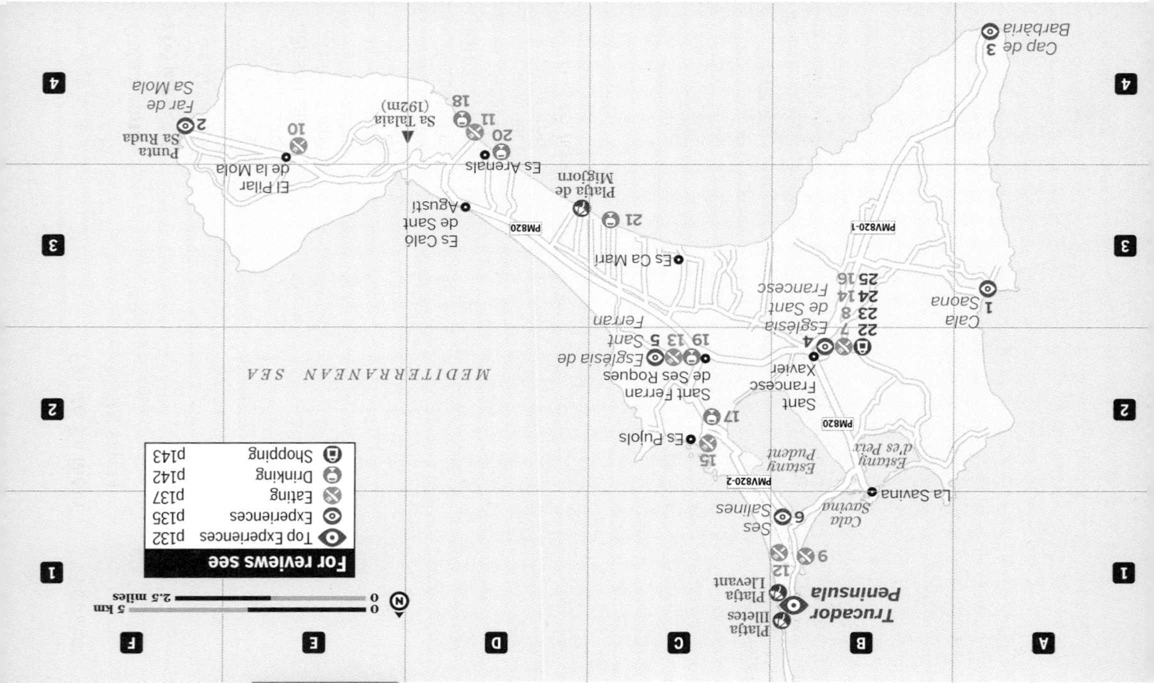

Formentera

MEDITERRANEAN SEA

For reviews see

⊙	Top Experiences	p132
⊙	Experiences	p135
⊗	Eating	p137
🍷	Drinking	p142
🛍	Shopping	p143

5 km
2.5 miles

Cala Savina

La Savina

Trucador Peninsula

Platja Illetes
Platja Llevant

12

9

Ses Salines 6

Estany Pudent

Estany d'es Peix

PMV820-2

15

Es Pujols

17

Sant Ferran de Ses Roques

Església de Sant Ferran

19 13 5

Es Caló de Sant Agustí

Es Arenals

20

11 18

Far de Sa Mola

2

Punta Sa Ruda

El Pilar de la Mola

10

Sant Francesc Xavier

PM820

Església de Sant Francesc

4

22 7

23 8

24 14

25 16

PMV820-1

Es Ca Marí

Platja de Migjorn

21

Sa Talaia (192m)

Cala Saona

1

Cap de Barbària

3

Experiences

Cala Saona BEACH

1  MAP P134, A3

Delectable Cala Saona is a fabulous west-coast beach where the water glows a startling shade of luminous turquoise and the powder-soft sand is salt white. Though popular, it isn't too developed, bar a couple of laid-back, good-vibe summer beach shacks, a kayak/SUP-rental stand and a hotel at the back of the bay. It's 3km west of the Sant Francesc–Cap de Barbària road and signposted 2km southwest of Sant Francesc.

In summer months, bus L5 runs here from La Savina (€1.80, 30 minutes, five daily) via Sant Francesc.

Far de Sa Mola LIGHTHOUSE

2 MAP P134, F4

Perched high over the Mediterranean, 2.5km southeast of El Pilar de la Mola, this 1861 clifftop lighthouse defines the eastern edge of the island, where gold-tinged cliffs cascade into cobalt waves in a sublime seascape. There's a monument to French writer Jules Verne (who used the end-of-the-world setting in one of his novels), along with the gorgeous Codice Luna (p137) cafe-restaurant.

Cap de Barbària NATURAL FEATURE

3 MAP P134, A4

The Balearics' southernmost point is an extraordinary lunarlike landscape of parched, rocky terrain that ultimately ends in the **Far**

Cala Saona

NITO/SHUTTERSTOCK ©

The Secret Behind Formentera's Clear Seas

If you find yourself wondering what makes Formentera's seas so electrically blue and brilliantly translucent (with a regular visibility of up to 50m), it's all down to their expansive seabed meadows of *posidonia* – an ancient, endemic Mediterranean seagrass known for its healing properties and rich production of oxygen. The Balearics' *posidonia* fields span a staggering 560 sq km, of which 80 sq km belongs to Formentera, where specimens can reach up to 100,000 years in age. Much of Formentera's *posidonia* is protected by the Unesco-listed **Parc Natural de Ses Salines** (p67).

Despite Formentera's ecofriendly tourism focus, its underwater ecosystems remain continuously at risk from marine pollution, irresponsible fishing and, in particular, the anchoring of boats. About 30% to 40% of its *posidonia* meadows have disappeared over the last few years. As a result, in 2017 island authorities launched the **Save Posidonia Project** (www.saveposidoniaproject.org), aiming to raise both awareness about and funds to protect these little-known, but fragile and essential, subsurface fields.

de Barbària, a 1970s lighthouse. Gazing out to sea and watching the waves crash against the cliffs below is captivating, especially at sunset. You have to park a little north of the lighthouse and walk the final 30 minutes or so. From the lighthouse, it's a 10-minute walk eastwards to the **Torre des Garroveret**, an 18th-century watchtower.

Església de Sant Francesc
CHURCH

4 MAP P134, B2

Looming over Sant Francesc's charming central square, with a stark whitewashed facade, the imposing village fortress-church dates from the early 18th century. It was the first church built when Formentera was resettled (after being abandoned in the 15th century), and cannons were mounted on its roof until 1860. (Plaça de Sa Constitució, Sant Francesc Xavier; ⏱hours vary)

Església de Sant Ferran
CHURCH

5 MAP P134, C2

Overlooking a humble little square, Sant Ferran's charming 19th-century church has an exposed-stone facade topped by a simple belfry. (Plaça de l'Església, Sant Ferran de Ses Roques; ⏱hours vary)

Ses Salines
LAGOON

6 MAP P134, B1

Protected by the Parc Natural de Ses Salines (p67), Formentera's salt pans haven't been used for salt production since 1984, though salt crystals still form in the pools naturally. Formed in Phoenician times, they now make up an important wetland zone for birdlife, including waders, gulls and the odd visiting flamingo. August to October is the best time to spot the latter.

Eating

Ca Na Pepa
CAFE €€

7 MAP P134, B2

Beside the church-fortress, this low-key cafe opens onto a delightful terrace with artily mismatched seating, shaded by brushwood and wrapped in bougainvillea. You could spend the entire day munching through the menu: croissants and omelettes for breakfast; wraps, pastas, salads and *bocadillos* (filled rolls) for lunch; and plenty of good meats and fish for dinner, plus excellent wines by the glass. (☏608 576060; www.canapepa.com; Plaça de Sa Constituciò 5, Sant Francesc Xavier; breakfasts €2-10, mains €9-17; ☉8.30am-11pm Apr-Oct; 🛜🅿)

Codice Luna
CAFE €

Right beside the La Mola lighthouse (p135), Codice Luna (see 2 ◉ Map p134, F4) is a beautifully designed cafe-restaurant, all whitewashed wood and an exquisite terrace opening up soul-stirring views of the Mediterranean. A small tapas-style menu includes tasty breakfast *tostadas* (topped toast) with local cheese, homemade cakes and platters of Iberian ham, and a DJ party celebrates every full moon in summer. (www.codiceluna.com; Far de Sa Mola; dishes €3.50-15; ☉10.30am-9pm Apr-Oct)

Ca Na Joana
MEDITERRANEAN €€€

8 MAP P134, B2

The magically seductive setting is half the appeal at this exquisitely restored 17th-century house (one of Formentera's most ancient): all blanched walls, exposed stone and candlelit tables on a bougainvillea-shaded terrace. Service is slick and efficient, and modern-Mediterranean dishes are elegantly prepared, from chilled carrot soup to squid-ink pasta, seafood specials and Iberian ham carved in the garden. (☏971 32 31 60; http://canajoanaformentera.es;

Platja de Migjorn

The island's entire southern arc is necklaced with sandy alabaster bays lapped by placid aqua-tinted waters, known collectively as Platja de Migjorn. Development (and clothes) are kept to a minimum on this swathe of coast, beloved of naturists and escapists. The best beaches are at the southeastern end around **Es Arenals**. Reached by a series of bumpy tracks branching off Formentera's main road (PM820), most of Migjorn's settlements are no more than a handful of houses, a couple of bar-restaurants and the odd hotel.

Carrer Berenguer Renart 2, Sant Francesc Xavier; mains €18-30; ⏱8pm-1am May-Oct)

Es Molí de Sal

SEAFOOD €€€

9 ⊗ MAP P134, B1

In a tastefully revamped mill, Es Molí de Sal boasts a lovely terrace, a stylish chill-out lounge and magnificent views across the sea to Ibiza's Es Vedrà. It serves some of Formentera's finest seafood, plus salads, pastas and meats. It's worth the splurge: try a rice dish (such as *arròs negre*) or the house speciality, *caldereta de llagosta* (lobster stew). (☎971 18 74 91; https://esmolidesal.es/en; Calle Afores; mains €20-45; ⏱1-11pm Apr–mid-Oct)

Can Toni

SPANISH €

10 ⊗ MAP P134, E4

An atmospheric, locally popular, century-old bar-restaurant in the heart of El Pilar de la Mola, hosting regular live music and flamenco nights. It's open year-round, dishing out home-cooked bites that range from salads, *bocadillos* and *tostadas* to tortilla and trays of cheeses and cold meats. (☎971 32 73 77; info@cantoniformentera.com; Plaça del Pilar; tapas €3-12; ⏱7pm-midnight Mon, 7am-midnight Tue-Fri, 9am-midnight Sat & Sun; 🛜)

Es Cupiná

SEAFOOD €€

11 ⊗ MAP P134, D4

On Platja de Migjorn's southeastern corner, and in business for 40 years, smart Es Cupiná is noted for its freshly cooked fish of the day. Paella, *fideuà* (paella-like fish-and-seafood noodle dish) and *bullit de peix* (fish stew) with *arròs a banda* (paella-like rice in fish stock; order ahead) are other specialities, or graze on tortilla, cured ham and the odd Asian-inspired creation such

---

Alternative Formentera

Like its sister Ibiza, Formentera has a strong counterculture heritage. After the Spanish Civil War, anti-Francoists were imprisoned in a concentration camp here – at least 58 prisoners are believed to have died between 1939 and 1942 – and some stayed on in postwar years. The camp's ruined remains, called **Es Campament**, are 2.5km northwest of the capital Sant Francesc Xavier on the island's main road (PM820). During the 1970s, many South American opponents to military rule fled to Formentera.

Bob Dylan, King Crimson (who recorded the track 'Formentera Lady') and Pink Floyd (whose album *More* features a Formentera windmill on its cover) were regulars on the island in the 1960s. The autobiographical *Dope in the Age of Innocence* by Damien Enright is an excellent account of the early hippy era on Formentera.

SIGFRID CAMPAMA PUIG/SHUTTERSTOCK ©

Església de Sant Francesc (p136)

as tuna tataki. (☎971 32 72 21; www.restaurantescupina.com; Platja de Migjorn; mains €13-24; ⏱1-4.30pm & 8pm-late May-Oct)

Restaurante Tanga SEAFOOD €€

12 ⊗ MAP P134, B1

Steps from the shimmering shore on Platja Llevant, long-standing Tanga delivers delicious seafood dishes, including grilled prawns, grouper, dorada and paella. The signature salad (mixed greens with slivers of salmon and cod) is a tasty starter, and there are also meat dishes (try the pork tenderloin with green-pepper sauce). (☎971 18 79 05; www.restaurantetanga.com; Platja Llevant; mains €15-28; ⏱8.30am-8pm May-Oct)

Can Forn SPANISH €€

13 ⊗ MAP P134, C2

Family-run Can Forn plates up authentic island cuisine and has a cosy old-school vibe. Go for dishes such as calamar a la bruta ('dirty calamari', with potato, Mallorcan sausage and squid ink), local lamb chops and habas (broad beans) fried with onions and garlic. (☎971 32 81 55; Carrer Major 39, Sant Ferran de Ses Roques; mains €10-16; ⏱1-3.30pm & 7.30-11pm Mon-Sat Apr-Nov)

S'Abeurada de Can Simonet SPANISH, INTERNATIONAL €€

14 ⊗ MAP P134, B2

An excellent-value set lunch menu (€11) and platters of cold meats and local cheeses are among the

SBELLOTT/SHUTTERSTOCK ©

Es Pujols

key attractions at this unpretentious, locally popular modern-rustic restaurant at the south end of town. Dinner is à la carte, with classics such as *patatas bravas* (potatoes in a spicy tomato sauce) and Iberian-ham croquettes balanced out by international flourishes, including hummus or vegetable samosas with red-curry sauce. (☑971 32 35 62; cansimonet.formentera@gmail.com; Carrer del Pla del Rei 111, Sant Francesc Xavier; tapas €5.50-13, mains €17-22; ☺noon-5pm & 8pm-midnight Mon-Sat)

Bocasalina   MEDITERRANEAN €€€

15 ✖ MAP P134, C2

This sophisticated glass-fronted waterside restaurant rustles up home-cooked pasta, spot-on seafood and steaks, and paellas and fresh fish for sharing. Dishes are

delicately prepared and elegantly presented, and there's a good selection of international-style tapas, too. Book a candlelit table on the romantic terrace overlooking the sea. (☑971 32 91 13; Passeig Marítim, Es Pujols; mains €18-30; ☺8.30am-1am mid-Apr–mid-Oct)

Café Matinal   CAFE €€

16 ✖ MAP P134, B2

A cheery cafe tucked into a slim alley just off Sant Francesc's main square, Matinal delights with its popular, well-priced home-cooked breakfasts fuelled by zingy fresh juices, free-range eggs, homemade jams and the like. Lunchtime bites range from lemon chicken and tofu fried rice to pastas with signature house sauces. (☑971 32 25 47; www.facebook.com/cafematinal;

Island Life: Orientation

Formentera has a population of just 12,120, and only three settlements that could realistically be called villages. The current number of inhabitants is actually a boom: as recently as 2005 it was just 7500. The island has always been sparsely populated; in fact, it was completely abandoned between the 15th century and 1697, due to attacks by North African raiders and plague outbreaks. Quite how it arrived at its name, said to be derived from the Latin word *frumentarium* (granary), is a mystery, as the local climate is unrelentingly arid and the rainfall low.

Sant Francesc Xavier & La Savina

Formentera's languorous microcapital, Sant Francesc Xavier, is a beautiful whitewashed village, with cafes on sunny corners and local life revolving around its central square, overlooked by an 18th-century **fortress-church** (p136). Barefoot-glam boutiques line its lively streets, which also host some excellent restaurants and hotels, and a 14th-century chapel. Just 3km northwest is the lakeside port-village of La Savina, where ferries from Ibiza dock.

Sant Ferran de Ses Roques & Es Pujols

Three kilometres east of Sant Francesc, sleepy, ordinary-looking Sant Ferran de Ses Roques has a handful of low-key cafes and restaurants, and an old sandstone **chapel** (p136). Back in the swingin' 1960s, however, it was a stop on the hippy trail – Bob Dylan jammed here and Pink Floyd had their guitars custom-made at a local workshop. The purple haze has lifted somewhat, but Sant Ferran still moves to a chilled-out beat, particularly at bohemian bar-restaurant **Fonda Pepe** (p142). Es Pujols, once a quiet fishing village and now the island's only real beach resort, lies 2km north, with rows of sun-bleached timber boat shelters lining its beachfront.

La Mola

El Pilar de la Mola, Formentera's southeasternmost village, is the only settlement on La Mola peninsula, an elevated limestone plateau where the coastline is mostly only accessible by boat. It has a white-walled 18th-century church and a sprinkling of cafe-restaurants and low-key boutiques, and is the final stop en route to the distant, evocative **Far de Sa Mola** (p135). The village springs to life for its twice-weekly **artisan-hippy market** (www.facebook.com/hippiemarketlamola; Avenida de la Mola 65, El Pilar de la Mola; ⊘4-9pm Wed & Sun May–mid-Oct).

Es Caló de Sant Agustí

Towards Formentera's southeast, the tiny fishing hamlet of Es Caló de Sant Agustí occupies a rocky cove ringed by faded timber boat shelters. It served as the port for communities in El Pilar de la Mola for centuries, and has a couple of excellent seafood restaurants. The coastline is jagged, but immediately west you'll find stretches of sparkling-white sand massaged by translucent water, known as **Ses Platgetes**.

Carrer Arxiduc Lluis Salvador 18, Sant Francesc Xavier; mains €12; ⏰8am-3pm Mon-Sat Easter-Oct)

Drinking

Tipic   CLUB

17 🚍 MAP P134, C2

Formentera only has one real club, but it's a good one: an intimate, Balearic-chic space that draws an increasingly good roster of DJs. It's said to have launched back in 1971 with a Pink Floyd gig. (📱676 885452; www.clubtipic.com; Avinguda Miramar 164, Es Pujols; €30-45; ⏰11pm-6am May–mid-Oct)

Chiringuito Bartolo   BAR

18 🚍 MAP P134, D4

Colourful Chiringuito Bartolo, at the far southeastern end of Platja de Migjorn, must be the world's tiniest beach bar, and is much loved by islanders. Sitting cheerfully on stilts, it hosts just a smattering of tables, and serves up drinks and snacks (€7 to €10) such as burgers and sandwiches to wander away with if there's nowhere to sit. (Platja de Migjorn; ⏰10am-sunset May-Oct)

Fonda Pepe   BAR

19 🚍 MAP P134, C2

A Formentera classic and said to be a former Dylan hang-out, Fonda Pepe is a knockabout bar that attracts a lively crowd of locals and travellers. It does great *pomadas* (shots of gin and lemon), along with island food (paellas, seafood, fresh fish; mains €12 to €22), and its walls are covered in photos from the good old hippy days. (Carrer Major 55, Sant Ferran de Ses Roques; ⏰8pm-1am Apr-Oct)

Piratabus   BAR

20 🚍 MAP P134, D4

A sun-bleached little beach shack that's something of a low-key Formentera legend, Piratabus is perfect for sipping a mojito (€10) and demolishing a few tapas (tortilla, nachos, potato salad; €5) or a *bocadillo* while drinking in the sensational coastal panoramas. (Platja de Migjorn; ⏰10am-sunset May-Oct)

Blue Bar
BAR

21 ⏻ MAP P134, C3

This psychedelic, sea-splashed bar is prime sunset stuff. Back in the '60s, word has it, it even played host to Bob Marley, Pink Floyd and King Crimson. Everything is blue – seats, sunshades, tables, toilets, walls. There's even a blue curaçao-based cocktail! Follow the signposted dirt track from Km 7.8 on the PM820. (☏666 758190; www.bluebarformentera. com; Platja de Migjorn; ⏱1pm-4am Apr-Oct; 📶)

Shopping

Muy
CLOTHING

22 🔒 MAP P134, B2

An exquisite concept store owned by Alessandro Negri, Formentera's most famous designer. The tastefully styled premises are graced by all the earthy, barefoot-style furnishings, organic-cotton clothing, gorgeous shoes and sandals, jewellery and accessories you could need. (☏971 32 16 22; Carrer Sant Joan 55, Sant Francesc Xavier; ⏱10am-2pm & 7-10pm May–mid-Oct)

Janne Ibiza
FASHION & ACCESSORIES

23 🔒 MAP P134, B2

Keep your summer look luxe, local and head-turning with this small local brand, which produces barely there, Formentera-chic bikinis (around €85) in statement designs such as leopard-print,

neon-pink, beachy-blue, flowery sequins and rainbow-striped crochet.

You can even get your bikini made-to-measure at the **Janne Ibiza boutique workshop** (www. janneibiza.es; Carrer Punta Prima 7 (Es Pujols); ⏱10.30am-2pm & 6pm-midnight) in Es Pujols. (☏971 32 89 63; www.janneibiza.es; Carrer d'Isidor Macabich 11, Sant Francesc Xavier; ⏱11.30am-2pm & 6.30-10.30pm)

Full Moon
CLOTHING

24 🔒 MAP P134, B2

Spot the bicycle by the sky-blue doors: this stylish, whitewashed inside-outside boutique stocks strappy sandals, straw hats, Balearic woven baskets, and chic kaftans, bikinis, scarves and bags. (☏971 32 23 76; Carrer Eivissa 6, Sant Francesc Xavier; ⏱10am-2pm & 6-10pm Mon-Sat, 10am-2pm Sun May-Sep)

Alma Gemela
SHOES

25 🔒 MAP P134, B2

'Alma Gemela' means 'soulmate' in Spanish and this lovely little boutique lives up to its name, specialising in glammed-up espadrilles (€60 to €70), which dangle in the garden and come in all kinds of colours (some glittery) and styles, including *payesa* (traditional and Formentera-made). (☏946 11 26 60; http://almagemelaformentera. com; Carrer d'Isidor Macabich 9, Sant Francesc Xavier; ⏱10am-2pm & 6pm-midnight May-Sep)

Survival Guide

Baleària ferry (p149) LARANIK/SHUTTERSTOCK ©

Before You Go

Book Your Stay

○ Book all Ibiza and Formentera accommodation well ahead.

○ Prices skyrocket from June to mid-September.

Best Budget

Es Alocs (www.hostal alocs.com;) A welcoming, no-frills beachside spot, with balcony-equipped rooms and a restaurant, on Ibiza's east coast.

Bar del Centro (http://barcentroformentera.com) Above a lively cafe-bar in Formentera's 'capital', this friendly, efficiently run guesthouse provides good-value rooms with antique tiling and shared bathrooms.

Best Midrange

Ca's Català (www.cascatala.com) A cheery, sparkling-white Santa Eulària guesthouse with a villa-like feel.

Vara de Rey (http://hibiza.com) Boho-cool

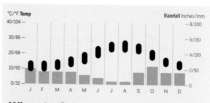

When to Go

High Season (mid-Jun–mid-Sep)

By August the islands are packed and humidity is high. Book well ahead for hotels and upscale restaurants.

Shoulder (Apr–mid-Jun & mid-Sep–Oct)

Accommodation prices significantly lower. Sea temperatures mild throughout September and October.

Low Season (Nov–Mar)

Mild winter days of 20°C aren't uncommon. Spectacular almond blossoms in February.

guesthouse in a 20th-century mansion in the heart of Ibiza Town.

Hostal Juanita (http://hostaljuanita.es) A gleaming, stripped-back Ibiza Town guesthouse with a splash of contemporary style.

Hotel Calador (www.calador-ibiza.com) Wake up to mind-bogglingly beautiful views of Es Vedrà in a sunny, low-key southwest-Ibiza hotel.

Hostal Rafalet (www.hostal-rafalet.com) With whistle-clean rooms and a seafood restaurant, this welcoming Es Caló *hostal* overlooks a small rocky harbour in Formentera.

La Dama d'Eivissa (www.ladamadeibiza.com) Bold colours, harbour views and a dash of boutique flair just back from Ibiza Town's port.

Best Top End

Urban Spaces (info@urbanspacesibiza.com) A unique Ibiza Town hotel, embellished with murals by top global street artists.

Los Enamorados

(https://losenamorado sibiza.com) A century-old Portinatx boat-house reimagined as an ultra-romantic hotel and restaurant with a tropical feel.

Gecko Beach Club

(www.geckobeachclub. com) Formentera slips into Ibiza's glam shoes at this beachfront beauty occupying an old farmhouse, with private plunge pools.

Hostal La Torre (www. latorreibiza.com) Boutiquey rooms, divine dining and an uncommercial music scene on seaside cliffs just north of Sant Antoni.

Es Marès (www.hoteles mares.com) This slinky boutique hotel exudes Mediterranean beach chic with its pool, tiled spa, all-white rooms

Sleeping Price Ranges

The following price ranges refer to a double room with bathroom:

€ less than €75

€€ €75–€200

€€€ more than €200

and modern-Balearic restaurant.

Rural Hotels (p12)

Many of Ibiza's and Formentera's top hotels are beautifully refurbished *agroturismes* given the boho-glam treatment.

Arriving in Ibiza

Aeroport d'Eivissa

Ibiza's **airport** (www.aena. es; Sant Jordi de ses Salines), 7km southwest of Ibiza Town, receives direct flights from mainland Spanish cities and many other UK and European destinations.

Taxi

○ There's a taxi rank right outside Ibiza airport's arrivals hall.

○ Between mid-July and the end of August, you may have to wait up to an hour for a taxi.

○ Typical fares are €18 to Ibiza Town, €26 to Sant Antoni and €35 to Sant Joan.

○ Check sample fares at www.ibizaairport.org.

Note that rates increase after 9pm.

○ Always use official taxis. Unlicensed 'pirate' drivers sometimes hang around the airport.

Bus

If you're travelling to anywhere other than Ibiza Town outside the May-to-October high season, you'll need to catch a bus to Ibiza Town, then change. Check **Ibiza Bus** (http://ibizabus. com).

L10 To/from Ibiza Town and Formentera Ferry Terminal (€3.50, every 20–30min 6am or 7am– midnight).

L9 To/from Sant Antoni, via Sant Josep (€4, half-hourly or hourly 6am–12.30am mid-May–mid-Oct).

L24 To/from Santa Eulària (€4, hourly 8am–midnight mid-May–mid-Oct).

Car & Motorcycle

International companies such as Hertz, Avis and Europcar have offices at the airport. Local car-hire companies often send someone to meet you at the airport with a car; otherwise, you'll have to use their complimentary shuttle buses, which can be time consuming.

Estació Marítima de Botafoc, Ibiza Town

Most long-distance ferries arriving/departing Ibiza use the new **Estació Marítima de Botafoc**, across the harbour from central Ibiza Town. Buses, taxis and shuttle boats hop across to the centre.

Ferries linking Ibiza Town with Formentera have their own **terminal** (off Avinguda de Santa Eulària), 400m north of central Ibiza Town.

La Savina, Formentera

Formentera has no airport. The only point of entry is the ferry port of La Savina, on the north side of the island, with excellent facilities including a **tourist office** (p151).

Taxi

From La Savina, typical taxi fares are €12 to Es Pujols and €15 to Platja de Migjorn.

Bus

Buses (p152) run from La Savina to Formentera's main villages.

Car, Motorcycle & Bicycle

You'll find car, bike and scooter rental outlets by the ferry terminal; rates barely vary between outlets. At the time of writing, island authorities are considering capping the number of rentals permitted on Formentera.

Getting Around

Bicycle

○ Designated cycle routes around Ibiza range from easy rides to tough climbs; routes on Formentera are mostly flat. Tourist offices have route maps.

○ **Ibiza MTB** (📞616 129929, 637 352929; www. ibizamtb.com; Carrer Joan Castelló 1, Sant Rafel de Sa Creu; ⏰10am-1pm & 5-8pm Mon-Fri, 10am-1pm Sat) rents quality bikes and offers guided rides.

Boat

Regular passenger ferries run between Ibiza Town and Formentera's La Savina,

---

Tourism Tax

In a bid to develop sustainable tourism and protect the fragile environment of a region inundated by mass tourism, the Balearics introduced a new 'tourism tax' in mid-2016. The tax applies to anyone aged 16 or over staying overnight, and is charged with each night of your accommodation (from camping to luxury hotel); from 2018 it will also apply to cruise day trippers. Exact rates vary according to the season (it's cheaper November to April), type of accommodation and length of stay. At the time of writing, rates were set to range from €1 to €4 per night for 2018.

with departures every 20 to 30 minutes May to October and reduced services November to April. Day-trip boats run from most Ibiza resorts and the Ibizan towns of Sant Antoni and Santa Eulària. There are substantial discounts for children.

Aquabus (www.aquabus ferryboats.com; ⏱6am-2am May-Oct, hours vary) One way/return €15/20; one hour.

Baleària (☎902 160180; www.balearia.com) One way €18 to €25, return €25 to €44; 30 minutes to one hour.

Mediterránea Pitiusa (☎971 31 44 61; www. mediterraneapitiusa.com; Formentera Ferry Terminal) One way/return €27/46; 30 minutes.

Trasmapi (☎971 31 07 11; www.trasmapi.com; Formentera Ferry Terminal) One way/return €27/47; 30 minutes.

Bus

○ Ibiza's bus networks are pretty efficient if you base yourself in one of the main towns, but services further afield are irregular or non-existent.

○ Check schedules through **Ibiza Bus** (http://ibizabus.com). Some services operate only May to October.

○ Fares are €1.55 to €4.

Car & Motorcycle

○ The islands' most remote spots cannot be reached on foot.

○ Many places (including rural hotels) are only accessible via dirt roads. Drive carefully and be aware that rental companies' insurance often won't cover damage to undercarriages.

○ Parking spots fill up quickly in summer; arrive early or consider alternative transport.

○ Rental companies have offices at the airport and around the island. Reliable companies include **Moto Luis** (☎971 34 05 21; www.motoluis.com; Avinguda de Portmany 17, Sant Antoni de Portmany; ⏱9am-9pm) and **Gold Car** (☎965 94 31 86; www.goldcar.es; Aeroport d'Eivissa; ⏱7am-11pm).

○ Cars can be in very short supply in summer and last-minute bookings may prove impossible; book ahead.

Discobus

Much cheaper than a taxi, the **Discobus** (www. discobus.es; per person €3 to €4; ⏱midnight-6am Jun-Sep) does all-night whirls, in various combinations, of the major clubs, bars and hotels in Ibiza Town, Platja d'en Bossa, Sant Rafel, Es Canar, Santa Eulària and Sant Antoni.

Taxi

○ Taxis are in very short supply in July and August; waits can be long.

○ There's a minimum €3 charge to flag down a taxi and €3.65 for a pick-up (€4.85 at night); then it's €1.09 per kilometre (€1.33 at night).

○ Taxi numbers:

Ibiza Town (☎971 39 84 83)

Santa Eulària (☎971 33 33 33)

Sant Antoni (☎971 34 37 64)

Sant Joan (☎971 33 33 33)

Sant Josep (☎971 80 00 80)

Ibiza Water Taxis

Many resorts, beaches and towns offer 'water taxi' connections from May to October. Routes include Sant Antoni to Cala Bassa, Cala Salada, Platges de Comte, Es Canar and Santa Eulària (via several east-coast beaches), and Ibiza Town to Santa Eulària and Platja d'en Bossa (via Figueretes). Companies include **Aquabus** (p149), **Santa Eulalia Ferry** (✆971 33 22 51; www.santaeulaliaferry.com; Passeig Marítim; ☽May-Oct) and **Cruceros Portmany** (✆971 34 34 71; www.crucerosportmany.com; Passeig de Ses Fonts; ☽May-Oct).

Walking

○ The Port Area of Ibiza Town and Dalt Vila are best explored on foot. There are fine promenades in Santa Eulària, Sant Antoni and Ibiza/Botafoc Marina.

○ Good hikes abound on the island. Check out **Walking Ibiza** (✆608 692901; www.walkingibiza.com) for guided walks to suit all levels.

Essential Information

Accessible Travel

○ Some museums, sights and offices, plenty of hotels and beaches and even the odd club have disabled access.

○ Pre-book adapted taxis through the **Federació Insular de Taxis de l'Illa d'Eivissa** (✆971 80 00 80; www.radiotaxiibiza.es).

○ As of 2017, Ibiza has over 20 beaches (plus a few more on Formentera) with access for people with disabilities, including boardwalks, ramps and, in some cases, amphibious chairs and adapted toilet and shower facilities. Among these are **Platja de Talamanca**, **d'en Bossa**, **Ses Salines**, **Cala d'Hort** and **Benirràs**. Tourist offices provide advice.

○ New hotels in Spain are required by law to have wheelchair-adapted rooms. Check the specifics of what this actually includes in each case.

Business Hours

Banks 8am–2pm Monday to Friday.

Post offices 8.30am–8pm Monday to Friday.

Restaurants Varies. In beach resorts, casual places open 8am–11pm. Elsewhere it's roughly 1pm–4pm and 8pm–11.30pm. Many close from November to April.

Shops 10am–9pm, often until midnight June to September.

Electricity

Type C
230V/50Hz

Health

Like everywhere, Spain has been impacted by the COVID-19 pandemic; check the latest entry requirements and local restrictions before travelling: https://travelsafe.spain.info.

Money

Credit cards are accepted in most hotels and restaurants, though don't expect to pay for sun loungers with plastic.

Public Holidays

New Year's Day 1 January

Epiphany 6 January

Balearics Day 1 March

Good Friday Late March/April

Easter Monday Late March/April

Labour Day 1 May

St Mary 5 August

St Ciriac 8 August

Assumption Day 15 August

Hispanic Day 12 October

All Saints Day 11 November

Constitution Day 6 December

Immaculate Conception 8 December

Christmas Day 25 December

Responsible Travel

The Balearic Islands, including Ibiza, are pushing forward long-term projects to transform tourism into a more sustainable, less seasonal industry. Check out http://www.illessostenibles.travel and https://www.ibizasostenible.com for details.

Overtourism

○ Help combat overtourism by visiting during off-season and staying longer.

○ Learn about sustainable living and local environmental projects at the pioneering Casita Verde ecology centre (p58).

○ Tourist rentals and illegal accommodation are driving up rents for the local population. Ensure your accommodation has an official licence number.

Support Local

○ Ibiza's markets are great spots to pick up fresh produce, often sold by local farmers.

○ Several organic-focused farms welcome visitors, while the islands' wineries are reviving traditional local grapes.

○ Enjoy an expert-led guided tour (such as with Ibiza Food Tours; https://ibizafoodtours.com) or learn a local craft (http://ibizacreativa.com).

Leave a Light Footprint

○ Use local buses to get around.

Money-Saving Tips

○ Use the **Discobus** (p149) for clubbing, and buses and bicycles for daytime explorations.

○ Skip peak season (late June to mid-September); hotel rates plummet outside these months.

○ Eating out can be expensive; *tostadas* and *bocadillos* are cheap cafe bites, while three-course lunch menus in simple restaurants are often €11 to €15.

Getting Around Formentera

Car, Motorcycle & Bicycle

○ Most travellers get around on two wheels. Bicycles (€8 to €10 per day), motorbikes (€30 to €40 per day) and cars (from €40) are available from rental outlets in La Savina (by the ferry terminal) and Es Pujols.

○ Flat Formentera is perfectly set up for cyclists. Island tourist offices provide maps of 28 dedicated cycle paths.

Bus

○ Formentera has a decent bus network run by **Autocares Paya** (http://busformentera.com). Regular bus tickets cost €1.80 to €2.55.

○ Schedules vary considerably according to the time of year; some services operate only mid-April to mid-October.

Taxi

Taxis are fairly expensive on Formentera. Taxi numbers:

La Savina (☏ 971 32 20 02)

Sant Francesc Xavier (☏ 971 32 20 16)

Es Pujols (☏ 971 32 80 16)

○ Hiking, cycling and horse-riding are rewarding, low-impact ways to explore..

○ Most of Ibiza's agroturismes combine soothing accommodation with a sustainable ethos.

Toilets

Unfortunately, toilets are few and far between. Popular beaches, including Talamanca and Ses Salines, have public toilets, but more remote coves don't. Generally it's best to use toilet facilities in cafes, restaurants and hotels.

Tourist Information

Ibiza

Turismo de Ibiza (☏ 971 30 19 00; http://ibiza.travel; Avinguda de Santa Eulària)

Ibiza Town (☏ 971 39 92 32; http://turisme.eivissa.es; Plaça de la Catedral)

Santa Eulària (☏ 971 33 07 28; www.santaeulalia.net; Carrer Mariano Riquer Wallis 4)

Sant Antoni (☏ 971 34 33 63; http://visit.santantoni.net; Passeig de Ses Fonts 1)

Sant Joan (☏ 971 33 30 75; Carrer de l'Ajuntament)

Formentera

La Savina (☏ 971 32 20 57; www.formentera.es; Carrer de Calpe, La Savina)

Es Pujols (☏ 971 32 89 97; www.formentera.es; Avinguda Miramar)

Sant Francesc Xavier (☏ 971 32 36 20; www.formentera.es; Plaça de Sa Constitució, Sant Francesc Xavier)

Language

Both Spanish (known as *castellano*, or Castilian) and Catalan (*català*, spoken in Catalonia) are official languages in Spain. Eivissenc is the native dialect of Catalan spoken on Ibiza and Formentera. You'll be perfectly well understood speaking Spanish in Ibiza and you'll find that most locals will happily speak Spanish to you, especially once they realise you're a foreigner. Here we've provided you with some Spanish to get you started, as well as some Catalan basics at the end.

Just read our pronunciation guides as if they were English and you'll be understood. Note that (m/f) indicates masculine and feminine forms.

To enhance your trip with a phrasebook, visit **lonelyplanet.com**. Lonely Planet iPhone phrasebooks are available through the Apple App store.

Basics

Hello.
Hola. — o·la

Goodbye.
Adiós. — a·dyos

How are you?
¿Qué tal? — ke tal

Fine, thanks.
Bien, gracias. — byen gra·thyas

Please.
Por favor. — por fa·vor

Thank you.
Gracias. — gra·thyas

Excuse me.
Perdón. — per·don

Sorry.
Lo siento. — lo syen·to

Yes./No.
Sí./No. — see/no

Do you speak (English)?
¿Habla (inglés)? — a·bla (een·gles)

I (don't) understand.
Yo (no) entiendo. — yo (no) en·tyen·do

Eating & Drinking

I'm a vegetarian. (m/f)
Soy vegetariano/a. — soy ve·khe·ta·rya·no/a

Cheers!
¡Salud! — sa·loo

That was delicious!
¡Estaba buenísimo! — es·ta·ba bwe·nee·see·mo

Please bring the bill.
Por favor nos trae la cuenta. — por fa·vor nos tra·e la kwen·ta

I'd like ...
Quisiera ... — kee·sye·ra ...

a coffee *un café* — oon ka·fe

a table for two *una mesa para dos* — oo·na me·sa pa·ra dos

a wine *un vino* — oon vee·no

two beers *dos cervezas* — dos ther·ve·thas

Shopping

I'd like to buy ...
Quisiera comprar ... — kee·sye·ra kom·prar ...

May I look at it?
¿Puedo verlo? — pwe·do ver·lo

How much is it?
¿Cuánto cuesta? — kwan·to kwes·ta

That's too/very expensive.
Es muy caro. — es mooy ka·ro

Emergencies

Help!
¡Socorro! · so·ko·ro

Call a doctor!
¡Llame a · lya·me a oon
un médico! · me·dee·ko

Call the police!
¡Llame a · lya·me a
la policía! · la po·lee·thee·a

I'm lost. (m/f)
Estoy perdido/a. · es·toy per·dee·do/a

I'm ill. (m/f)
Estoy enfermo/a. · es·toy en·fer·mo/a

Where are the toilets?
¿Dónde están · don·de es·tan
los baños? · los ba·nyos

Time & Numbers

What time is it?
¿Qué hora es? · ke o·ra es

It's (10) o'clock.
Son (las diez). · son (las dyeth)

morning	*mañana*	ma·nya·na
afternoon	*tarde*	tar·de
evening	*noche*	no·che
yesterday	*ayer*	a·yer
today	*hoy*	oy
tomorrow	*mañana*	ma·nya·na

1	*uno*	oo·no
2	*dos*	dos
3	*tres*	tres
4	*cuatro*	kwa·tro
5	*cinco*	theen·ko
6	*seis*	seys
7	*siete*	sye·te
8	*ocho*	o·cho
9	*nueve*	nwe·ve
10	*diez*	dyeth

Transport & Directions

Where's ...?
¿Dónde está ...? · don·de es·ta ...

What's the address?
¿Cuál es la · kwal es la
dirección? · dee·rek·thyon

Can you show me (on the map)?
¿Me lo puede · me lo pwe·de
indicar · een·dee·kar
(en el mapa)? · (en el ma·pa)

I want to go to ...
Quisiera ir a ... · kee·sye·ra eer a ...

What time does it arrive/leave?
¿A qué hora · a ke o·ra
llega/sale? · lye·ga/sa·le

I want to get off here.
Quiero bajarme · kye·ro ba·khar·me
aquí. · a·kee

Catalan – Basics

Good morning.
Bon dia. · bon dee·a

Good afternoon.
Bona tarda. · bo·na tar·da

Good evening.
Bon vespre. · bon bes·pra

Goodbye.
Adéu. · a·the·oo

Please.
Sisplau. · sees·pla·oo

Thank you.
Gràcies. · gra·see·a

You're welcome.
De res. · de res

Excuse me.
Perdoni. · par·tho·nee

I'm sorry.
Ho sento. · oo sen·to

How are you?
Com estàs? · kom as·tas

Very well.
(Molt) Bé. · (mol) be

Behind the Scenes

Send Us Your Feedback

We love to hear from travellers – your comments help make our books better. We read every word, and we guarantee that your feedback goes straight to the authors. Visit **lonelyplanet.com/contact** to submit your updates and suggestions.

Note: We may edit, reproduce and incorporate your comments in Lonely Planet products such as guidebooks, websites and digital products, so let us know if you are happy to have your name acknowledged. For a copy of our privacy policy visit **lonelyplanet.com/legal**.

Acknowledgements

Cover photograph: Ibiza Town, LUNAMARINA/Getty Images © Back cover photograph: Espalmador, Anton Petrus/Getty Images ©

Isabella's Thanks

Gracias to Louis, Andrew, Becky, Doug, Val, Andy, Martin and Iain. Extra special *gracias* to my fabulous Spain co-writers, especially John, Gregor, Duncan and Brendan.

This Book

This 3rd edition of Lonely Planet's *Pocket Ibiza* guidebook was researched and written by Isabella Noble, who also wrote the previous edition. This guidebook was produced by the following:

Destination Editor Tom Stainer

Senior Product Editors Angela Tinson, Genna Patterson

Product Editors Andrea Dobbin, Sandie Kestell, Amanda Williamson

Senior Cartographer Anthony Phelan

Book Designer Norma Brewer

Assisting Editors Janet Austin, Andrew Bain, Alex Conroy, Alexander Knights, Gabrielle Stefanos

Assisting Cartographer Rachel Imeson

Cover Researcher Ania Bartoszek

Thanks to Joe Bindloss, Gemma Graham, Paul Harding, Liz Heynes, Sonia Kapoor, Tanya Parker, Martine Power, Alison Ridgway, Dianne Schallmeiner, Fiona Flores Watson

Index

See also separate subindexes for:

⊗ Eating p158

◔ Drinking p159

✪ Entertainment p159

🔒 Shopping p159

Our Writer

Isabella Noble

English-Australian on paper and Spanish at heart, travel journalist Isabella has been wandering the globe since her first round-the-world trip as a one-year-old. Having grown up in an Andalucian village, she is a bilingual Spain specialist, and also writes about India, Thailand, Greece, the UK, Australia and beyond for Lonely Planet, *Condé Nast Traveller*, the *Telegraph*, the *Guardian*, GeoPlaneta, Ink magazines, BA *High Life* and others. Isabella has written many Lonely Planet Spain guides (from Andalucía to Pocket Barcelona), is a Telegraph Spain expert and writes in Spanish too. She has also contributed to Lonely Planet *India, South India, Thailand, Thailand's Islands & Beaches, Great Britain, Greece* and *Greek Islands*, and authored *Pocket Phuket*. Find Isabella on Twitter and Instagram (@isabellamnoble) or at https://isabellanoble.com.

Published by Lonely Planet Global Limited
CRN 554153
3rd edition – Sep 2022
ISBN 978 1 78701 626 2
© Lonely Planet 2022 Photographs © as indicated 2022
10 9 8 7 6 5 4 3 2 1
Printed in Malaysia